*Unstoppable Me:
Empowering Diabetes Care*

Copyright © 2024 by Lorraine Sweeney

All Rights Reserved. No part of this book may be reproduced, distributed, or transmitted in any form or by any means, including photocopying, recording, or other electronic or mechanical methods, without the prior written permission of the publisher, except in the case of brief quotations embodied in critical reviews and certain other non-commercial uses permitted by copyright law.

Author's Note

This book is not a medical journal or meant to give or replace medical advice.

This is my story of 28 years of living with Type 1 diabetes and the challenges I have experienced, but more importantly, how technology is changing the landscape of Type 1 diabetes, and for you not to be afraid. To embrace it.

This book was written to share and ultimately inspire anyone who is on a journey to achieving better control of their diabetes and living a fuller life. As my journey will show you, I have come a long way; with the advancement of technology, we have all come a long way in the treatment of diabetes.

No matter where you are on your journey to achieving control, this book can inspire you. If your journey has just begun, I am very hopeful that achieving control will be much easier than when my journey started. If you are well into the journey and are thinking about embracing some of the new technologies, I hope to be that beacon of light beckoning you forward.

Lorraine

Table of Contents

PART ONE - My Journey With Diabetes

Chapter 1:	It Started in the Pub!	7
Chapter 2:	Life Before Diabetes	11
Chapter 3:	Navigating the Medical Maze	17
Chapter 4:	Two Men Walked into My Life	23
Chapter 5:	A Chance Encounter	30
Chapter 6:	Navigating Life's Rollercoaster: From Loss to Liberation	35
Chapter 7:	The T Slim Pump - How AI Helped Change my Life	47
Chapter 8:	Empowered Living: Navigating the Three Pillars of Control	60

PART TWO - Tips For Making Your Life Easier While Living With Diabetes.

Chapter 9:	Sleep	66
Chapter 10:	Manifesting, Gratitude & all Things Roxie Nafousi	70
Chapter 11:	Exercise	76
Chapter 12:	Food	84
Chapter 13:	More Hints and Tips to Help You on Your Journey	119
Chapter 14:	Talking About Diabetes - Language Matters	123
Chapter 15:	Final Words – My Formula for Wellness	138

Quote

I do not love to work out, but if I stick to exercising every day and put the right things in my mouth, then my diabetes just stays in check.

Halle Berry

PART ONE

My Journey With Diabetes

Chapter 1
It Started in the Pub!

It all started on a winter Friday evening in early December 1996. We had a tough week at work, and the team loved nothing more than piling into the local pub for some beers to decompress. I was the first at the bar, buying everyone a drink. At age 28, I was a senior partner in the company and life was good. I loved my work; I worked hard, played hard, and enjoyed socialising with the team. My plan for tomorrow was Christmas shopping for my family. A lovely weekend ahead.

About an hour later, my doctor called and suggested I go to A&E immediately. The blood tests were back, and they were very concerning. She indicated that she had already faxed the results to the office, and I needed to go straight to A&E to present them.

Feeling very concerned, the team and I returned to the office to check out the test results.

At the time, my sister-in-law was a ward sister in a hospital, so I called her and read the medical information from the fax. She was a little confused.

"OK, have you lost a lot of weight?" she asked.
I replied, "Yes, I'm delighted with the amount of weight I've lost. I've even won slimmer of the week at Weight Watchers."
Poignantly, she asked if I was thirsty and sleeping all the time.
Exhaustion is always part of my hectic lifestyle, so I thought nothing of this.

My sister-in-law felt it was unlikely that my blood sugar of 48 could be so high and that I was still functioning. We decided I could go home, have a glass of wine and my takeaway curry as planned, and pop into the hospital the next day on my way to complete my festive shopping. Our view was that the doctor was being slightly dramatic and that my blood sugar levels were incorrect.

I went to the hospital the next day for blood tests. Many doctors came in to examine me and asked if I felt okay. I reassured them that I felt fine, but they were surprised by my blood sugar levels. This marked the beginning of my journey with type 1 diabetes.

The hospital had originally specialised in TB, and as there were no rooms available in the main building I was admitted and placed in an isolation unit. Since it was the weekend, there were very few doctors available. I was administered insulin and given numerous leaflets to help me understand how my life would change and the do's and don'ts of diabetes. I received instructions on what I could no longer eat or drink and was warned of the potential consequences. I was given large syringes and oranges and told to practice how to inject myself. It was hard to believe what was happening to me.

My family was shocked but supportive. One brother was helping to plan my great escape for early Monday morning, while another was reminding me that my long, lazy, hazy, red wine lunches were now officially over! I was so angry and frustrated that I felt like throwing my (practice) oranges at every visitor. I was supposed to be shopping for Christmas presents, catching up with pals later, and enjoying the festivities.

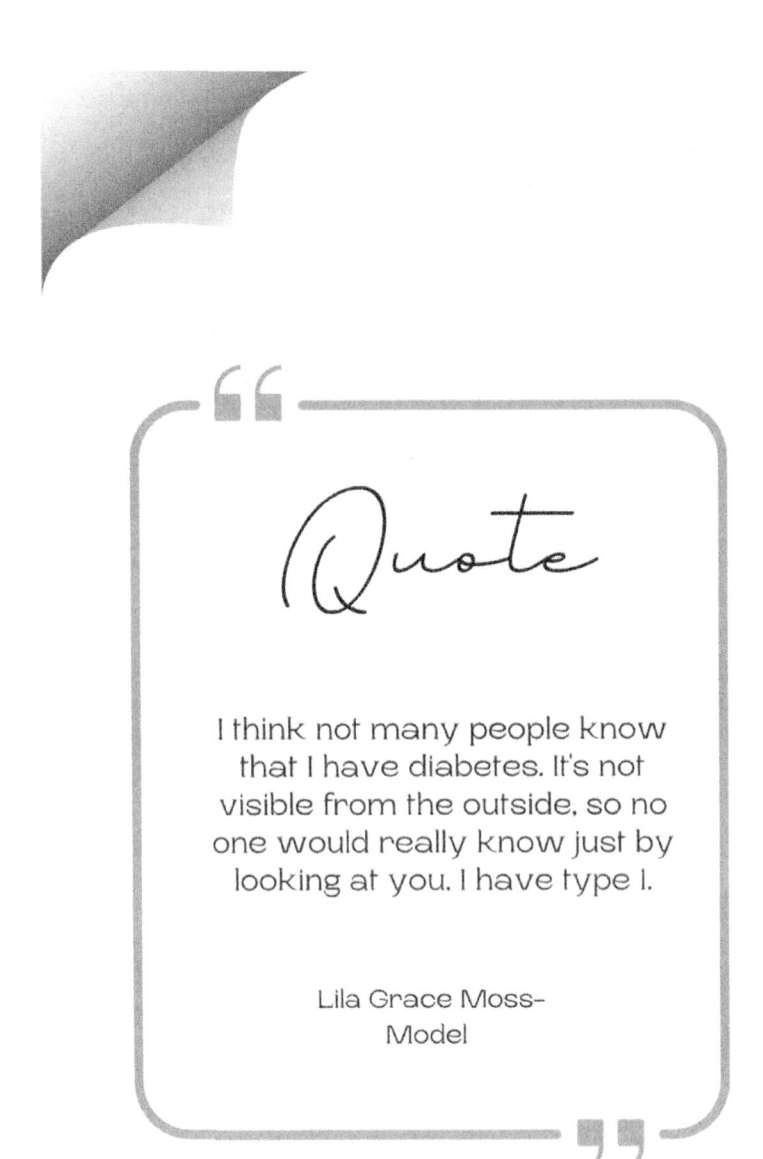

Quote

I think not many people know that I have diabetes. It's not visible from the outside, so no one would really know just by looking at you. I have type 1.

Lila Grace Moss-
Model

Chapter 2

Life Before Diabetes

I was born in 1968 and am the tenth of eleven children. I have seven brothers and three sisters. And yeah, life was chaotic, but great chaos and lots of fun. I went to boarding school at 12, and I loved it. I couldn't believe that I could go to school and have all my pals around me at all times. I definitely would have been a social bunny; making people laugh was my mission.

When I was around 20 years of age, I was involved in a hit-and-run car accident. I was a passenger in the car. The other driver was drunk; he shouted some words at us, jumped back in his car and drove off. We were stunned. The police were called, statements were given, and my pal's parents came to collect us.

The next day, I knew I was in trouble. I could hardly move out of the bed, and it was clear my neck and back were in complete spasm. It was a stark realisation that I was severely injured in the accident.

After years of pain and alternative treatments, I was left with no choice but to have spinal surgery. I had a spinal fusion operation about two years later. I was terrified going in for the surgery. My parents were under no illusion of how extensive this surgery was.

I was in a full-body plaster cast from neck to hip for over a year. I was totally dependent on my mother to do everything from washing my hair to tying my shoelaces and everything in between. This was a really difficult time given that I was so independent in boarding school. But I tried to continue to live an everyday life, attend college, and even go for a few drinks with my friends.

I had to think long and hard about a career after the surgery. But one thing I knew for sure: this would not define me. I focused on getting fitter and stronger and getting my life back on track.

After a long 18 months, I went from being utterly dependent on my mother to being completely independent. I had bought my first house, and I was delighted with myself. Life was looking up.

I started building a great career as a Management Consultant and enjoying life. I was committed to my job and loved to work morning, noon, and night.

"I worked hard and was thrilled when I became a partner in a management consultancy firm. This wasn't just a job for me; it was a passion that fueled every waking moment. The excitement of presenting and working with senior management levels in various organisations, delving into the intricacies of the financial and IT sectors, and collaborating with brilliant minds all contributed to a fulfilling professional life. In my eyes, I had a full and happy life; I worked hard, played hard, earned a great salary, and life was good.".

The demands of my work were intense, but I embraced the challenges with enthusiasm and dedication. Travelling for work became second nature to me, and each trip presented an opportunity to broaden my horizons and connect with successful individuals from different walks of life. My interactions with these people enriched my understanding of the business world and inspired me to strive for greater heights in my career.

Although my profession was demanding, I made sure to maintain a healthy balance between work and play. Spending time with my loved ones was very important to me. Whether it was a calm family dinner or a thrilling trip with friends, these experiences enriched my life beyond the corporate world. It's worth noting that I was also renowned for hosting excellent parties.

The chapter of my life at the top of my career was a tapestry woven with threads of diligence, passion, and adventure. It was a time of growth, discovery, and fulfilment, during which I embraced the corporate world's challenges and the joys of personal exploration. I loved the home that I had purchased by the sea, and I was truly very happy.

In 1996, around nine years after my initial back injury, I experienced a relapse. It happened over the May bank holiday weekend when I was supposed to go away with some friends. Unfortunately, I found myself unable to move and ended up on the floor. I was admitted to hospital on Tuesday and had to spend a week on an epidural drip. It was frustrating to have to take time off work and deal with the slow pace of my recovery. Looking back, I know it was my lifestyle that played a role in my relapse.

After leaving the hospital in June, I had a clear plan to improve myself, lose weight, join a slimming club, and make positive changes in my life. "Balance" was a new word for me!

I started to lose weight dramatically. I couldn't believe it. I was delighted. I was winning the slimmer of the week every week, losing three, four, or five pounds without even thinking about it. I was thrilled.

An issue that concerned me was recurring infections. Weekly prescribed antibiotics were taking their toll on me. About four months later, my doctor suggested referring me to a gynaecologist, who immediately recommended that I get my blood checked for diabetes first.

I had to take the morning off work to go for these tests. I reassured my business partner that I didn't have diabetes, even though I wasn't even sure what diabetes was. It was a Friday morning, and the plan was to fast, take some blood, eat cake, and then come back an hour later for more blood tests. The doctor said she would notify me of the results the following week. It sounded like a fun Friday - go and eat cake!

Quote

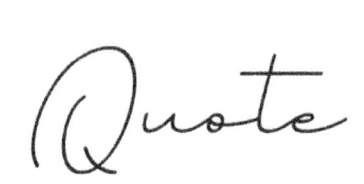

Diabetes sounds like you're going to die when you hear it. I was immediately frightened. But once I got a better idea of what it was and that is was something I could manage myself, I was comforted.

Nick Jonas- Singer & Songwriter

Chapter 3

Navigating the Medical Maze

While lying on the hospital bed, I had a lot of questions that needed answers. I was trying to understand why this happened to me. I wasn't feeling sorry for myself; I was trying to figure out how it had happened.

Type 1 diabetes is believed to be caused by an autoimmune reaction where the body mistakenly attacks itself. This attack destroys the beta cells in the pancreas that produce insulin. This process can continue for months or even years before any symptoms become noticeable. In layman's terms, it is also known as the silent killer. It can be hereditary, but scientists believe it is also caused by genes and environmental factors, such as viruses or shock, that may trigger the disease. I started to process which may have triggered my disease.

I had a car accident, followed by surgery, followed by high dosages of steroids. Trauma for seven years. My diagnosis was an accumulation of events and experiences, none of which were in my control or, indeed, my fault.

On Monday morning, with the assistance of my brother, I discharged myself from the hospital and we located my first diabetic consultant. I received treatment as a day patient and travelled to the diabetes clinic daily. As I dealt with the intricacies of managing diabetes, I faced a variety of reactions and opinions from those in my surroundings.

"My uncle is a raving diabetic; you're not bad at all."

"Have you the fat person type or the slim person type?"

"You don't look like you have diabetes."

"Did you eat loads of chocolate when you were younger?"

"Please don't check your blood sugars in front of the children."

"Please don't inject at the dinner table."

The insensitive remarks and misconceptions I faced added to the weight of managing my health while juggling a demanding career.

Even in front of friends and family, if I had a sugar low, the suggestion to rescue the situation was to give me insulin, or if I was on a sugar high and not feeling well, a Mars bar was prescribed. I appreciated the positive sentiment, but there was no real understanding behind the remarks.

At work, I often found myself concealing the reality of my condition. Life consisted of performing delicate balancing acts and concealing all the time what was actually going on. Discretely checking my sugars, administering insulin and high-speed snacking whilst running events for demanding businesses.

Exhausted after a day's work. I was in bed by 6 pm. I would regularly have a sugar low in the middle of the night and end up lying on the kitchen floor, eating everything that I could find. I was simply terrified of dying.

Eventually, I would go back to sleep but would have to drag myself out of bed the next morning to get to work. I was beyond exhausted. I became an expert at hiding behind my smile and personality. This was my cycle for years.

The search for a doctor who could truly understand my struggles and provide the support I needed was fraught with challenges. One doctor suggested, "You are an intelligent girl; you will figure things out yourself", which seemed impossible.

He was a well-respected consultant, and neither of us spoke the same language. I was an emotional wreck, unable to grasp what was happening to me, and he was a professor who couldn't understand what I didn't understand! His off-the-cuff comments left me adrift in a sea of uncertainty. I decided it was best to divorce him and move to a hospital close to my home and hopefully to a new doctor who was going to help.

The next consultant was on the other extreme. He was so strict that he would throw you out if you did not attend the clinic with a full set of numbers. Everyone who knows me knows that numbers are not part of my skill set. He would expect a spreadsheet full of data to include what time I ate, my blood sugars, how much insulin I took, why, and much more. So, I fudged all these numbers, which had zero relevance to my blood sugars. They just looked good.

I stayed with him for two years, and during that time, I was trying to juggle a pressurised career, hide my diabetes from everyone, manage roller coaster sugars and try to get a handle on what to do. I grappled with the rigid protocols of a clinic that seemed disconnected from the realities of managing diabetes on a day-to-day basis.

I knew I had to find a doctor who could genuinely connect with me, understand my struggles, and provide the help I needed.

It was a chance encounter with a compassionate nurse that would ultimately lead me to a doctor who would change the trajectory of my diabetes management. A new physician was returning to Ireland from the UK with a reputation for empathy and understanding and offered a glimmer of hope in what had been a tumultuous healthcare journey thus far. The nurse asked if she should put my name down for his clinic; I was delighted.

Quote

People think it's hard to cut out sugar, but it can be done. You just have to put some effort in.

Halle Berry

Chapter 4

Two Men Walked into My Life

1999 was a great year. The two most important men walked into my life. The first was husband Ray, whom I met in January. I was 31 years of age, and Ray was 34. We quickly knew this relationship was strong: openness and honesty were key. I told Ray about my situation, and he was instantly supportive. He was the first to show me a genuine understanding of myself. So, when friends or family would suggest going to the bathroom to inject or check my blood sugars, Ray would stand by and support me. Nothing was an issue.

The second person to enter my life that year was Dr O'Shea. During our first meeting, I realised he "got me." He listened to my story and assured me that he would help. I left the meeting feeling relieved, knowing I was in safe hands. Over the next 23 years, we would navigate this journey together.

Dr O'Shea introduced me to a new perspective on diabetes management. 90% of type 1 diabetics focused on food and insulin, which would result in reasonable control.

I realised that my control relied on **food, insulin, and emotion.** The highs and lows of my life played a significant role in managing my blood sugar levels. My life was a rollercoaster, and I wore my heart on my sleeve. I quickly realised It was going to be a big challenge to get my diabetes and life under control.

Dr O 'Shea and I worked together over the next few years on tools and building blocks to help me manage my new life.

The first change was my introduction to a **Sliding Scale Framework** for insulin. At long last, I had a structure. So delighted was I that I laminated this paper and had it with me all the time. I would check my blood before I ate, and pending my results, I would take the allocated amount of insulin. This was a whole new approach for me and one I loved. I wanted to gain control of my life and health, but I also wanted to show Dr O'Shea that I was willing to listen and do everything he suggested.

We started to work together as a team. I would research, and every time we met, he would ask, "So what do we have to discuss today, Lorraine?" I would have some new information or approaches to improving the life of a person with type 1 diabetes. Google was my best friend, and Dr O'Shea was my sounding board.

Together, we would discuss, and nine times out of ten, we would go for it. I was always willing to give new things a try.

Sometimes, it wouldn't work. Like the time I had a severe reaction to a new human-based insulin. I gained a stone within a month and was so utterly depressed. I had never felt anything like this deep, dark cloud over my head that I couldn't shake off. I was away on holiday on the Amalfi Coast with Ray, and all I could do was cry. I had no idea what was wrong with me. I couldn't put my finger on it. When I came back, Dr O'Shea and I discussed it, and I was immediately taken off it and placed on another medication. The black cloud floated away.

I was selected to attend one of the first DAFNE (Dose Adjustment for Normal Eating) courses. This was a total game-changer. The inclusion of the words "For Normal Eating" had a positive impact.

The DAFNE approach involves testing blood glucose just before and two hours after each meal and calculating quick-acting insulin doses according to blood glucose levels and carbohydrate intake. It provides flexibility in eating. It was very intensive but fantastic. However, following the regime was a full-time job. Checking and recording blood sugars, counting carbohydrates for the meal, taking insulin, eating, then checking and recording blood sugars again.

Rinse and repeat three times a day. This new routine helped me to understand that diabetes management is a full-time job that needs full attention every day of my life.

For years, I would work so hard and tried desperately to be a regular member of a gym, participate in a slimming club, yoga, and everything else possible to keep my weight down and stay fit, healthy, and calm. I lived a roller coaster life of blood sugar and control, but I always had a determination. I showed up at every event with the best attitude possible and always had a sense of humour. No one knew, nor did they want to know what was really going on.

A year into marriage, Ray and I were told by Dr O'Shea that it was highly unlikely I would be in a position to carry a baby. My diabetes was very brittle. Of course, everyone is different, which is one of the main reasons I wanted to write this book. I had met a few Mums who had given birth to healthy babies and had type 1 diabetes. So why couldn't I do it? It was Dr O'Shea who suggested we get a second opinion.

Unfortunately, it was confirmed. I was advised, "With brittle diabetes and very little or no control, a spinal fusion……I am highly recommending that under no circumstances should you have a child". It would have been a risk to both the baby and me.

This was a huge blow for both of us. As one of eleven siblings with over thirty nieces and nephews, I took it for granted that family would follow our recent marriage. Always a forward-thinking and practical person, Ray remained focused on what was truly important, and we made the most difficult decision any newly married couple could ever make. We were both very sad.

Nevertheless, a melody of resilience emerged—a testament to our strength and commitment. In the absence of our own progeny, we found solace in the laughter of nieces and nephews and the threads of familial bond.

Luckily, Ray always travelled extensively for work. We have seen beautiful parts of the world and have had amazing fun. However, our adventures were also encompassed by sugar highs and sugar lows. Dramatic incidents, including collapsing in toilets, falling over, and even being rescued by rangers on our honeymoon! – That's another story for another day!! However, these stories became fodder for our dinner party repertoire. This was our life.

I threw myself into my business, which went from strength to strength. I was on full speed. My father's expression, "Your health is your wealth," was so true; however, in my eyes, wealth was measured in your bank account.

I never thought about the consequences. I was successful and had a fabulous social life, but there was zero balance in my world.

In 2009, I received a call to say my sister was seriously ill. Jackie had been diagnosed with a brain tumour. Jackie was my eldest sister and touched so many people's hearts. An excellent, accomplished schoolteacher, mum, sister, friend and wife. Jackie put up a great fight, and we were totally devastated in 2011 when she passed away. It was the first time I truly had experienced deep, raw grief like a hole had been gouged out of me.

After Jackie's death, I knew I had to change my life and find something that would help bring greater control to my diabetes.

I was constantly researching. The internet was my new best friend. I searched for any news articles regarding diabetes. Armed with the latest update from the United States, I attended my bi-annual meetings with Dr. O'Shea, searching for a miracle.

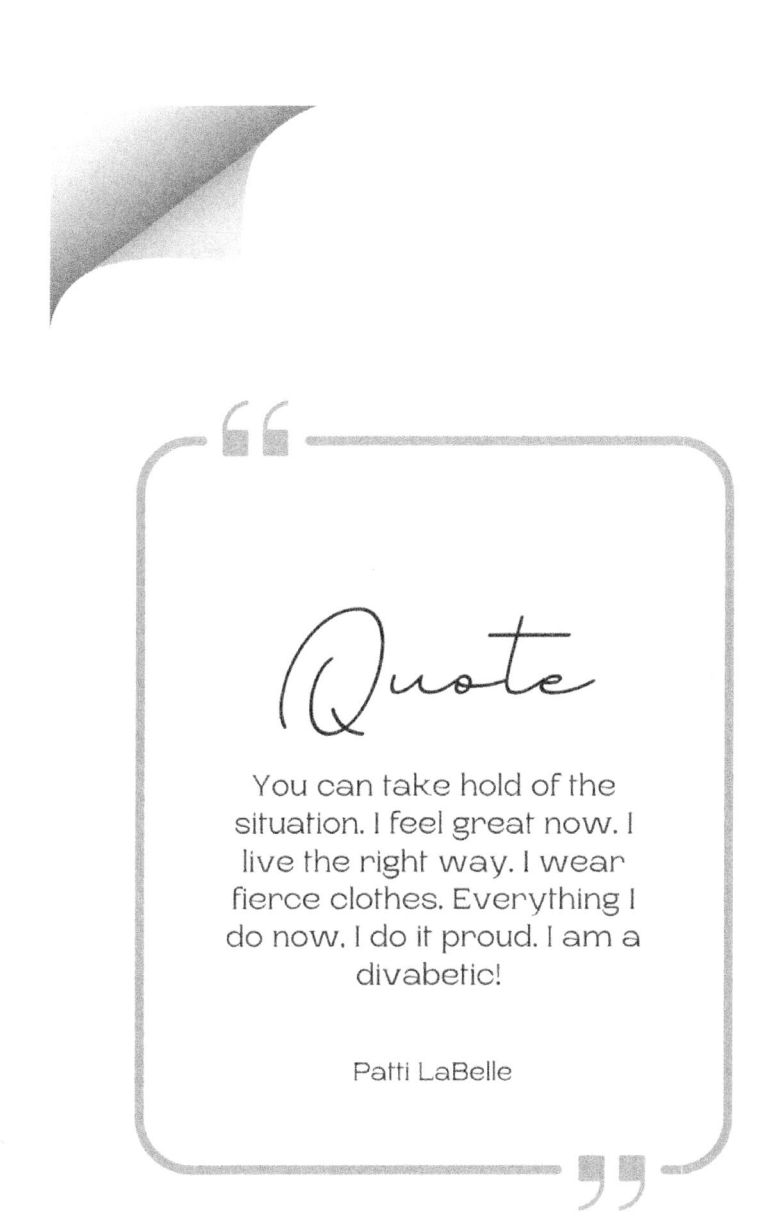

Quote

You can take hold of the situation. I feel great now. I live the right way. I wear fierce clothes. Everything I do now, I do it proud. I am a divabetic!

Patti LaBelle

Chapter 5

A Chance Encounter

I was returning to Ireland from a business training event and sat in a bustling airport, anxiously awaiting the departure of my delayed flight. Little did I know that a chance encounter would change the course of my journey with diabetes. The storm outside mirrored the whirlwind of emotions within me as fear of flying gripped my every thought. I always had this irrational fear of flying – but in this instance, it was off the charts, and I got myself completely wound up and anxious. The flight delay was due to a raging storm, and I secretly hoped there would be no take-off till calm returned. It was amid this turbulence that a kind-hearted gentleman approached me; he seemed to recognise my distress and gently struck up a conversation, offering words of reassurance and understanding.

The stranger, Mr. Jan DeVries, extended an invitation to sit with him during our seven hours of unexpected delay. Our conversation meandered through various topics, eventually leading to the serendipitous revelation that I had type 1 diabetes, and he was working on a book about type 1 diabetes. As fate would have it, we ended up seated together on the flight, and he continued to offer words of comfort and support throughout the journey.

During this time, to my surprise, he suggested that I visit his clinic the following morning, expressing a genuine interest in having me contribute to his work. Intrigued and hopeful, I stepped off the plane and shared the extraordinary encounter with Ray, excitement tinged with a hint of disbelief at the unexpected turn of events.

The following morning, I found myself at Mr. Jan DeVries' clinic, only to discover that this generous stranger was a renowned alternative doctor and a trusted physician to the Queen. He came once a month to run his clinic in Ireland, and there must have been close to one hundred people in the queue waiting to see him that morning. I was brought in to see Mr. De Vries and observed his compassion shine through as he welcomed me into his world of holistic healing. Monthly visits to Mr. DeVries' clinic became a cornerstone of my journey.

In the days and months that followed, Mr. DeVries' expert guidance and support became instrumental in helping me navigate the complexities of my emotions and the impact on my diabetes, as well as the enormity of managing life around it.

His holistic approach to healthcare and unwavering compassion were guiding lights, empowering me to embrace alternative treatments and a newfound sense of balance and direction in my life.

One particularly touching and lasting aspect of my interaction with Mr. DeVries was when he dedicated a chapter in his book to our shared encounter. The chapter began with the simple yet profound words, "I met this highly strung lady in Stanstead airport."

The chapter dedicated to our chance encounter in his book was not just a testament to our unlikely connection but a reminder of the profound impact that acts of kindness and understanding can have on our journey towards healing. It was through this chance encounter that I learned the power of vulnerability and the transformative potential of human connection in navigating life's challenges – in this case, transcending the boundaries of conventional patient-doctor relationships.

I hope that by sharing this chapter of my life, others may find solace in the knowledge that even amid uncertainty, there exists the potential for life-altering connections that illuminate the path forward.

Transitioning to Dr. O Shea and meeting with Dr. Jan De Vries marked a pivotal moment in my relationship with diabetes. Finally, I found healthcare providers who not only possessed the medical expertise to guide me but also treated me with the respect and compassion I had longed for. Under their care, I began to navigate the intricate dance of managing my health while pursuing a career that demanded my utmost attention and energy.

I cannot stress enough how important it is to ensure that you get the right team around you. Don't be afraid to ask any questions. Be curious. Understand that it's not one type of treatment or the other; you should take a holistic approach. Both medical and alternative medicine can work well together.

Reflecting on these experiences, I have come to appreciate the profound impact of a strong doctor-patient relationship in the realm of diabetes management. Beyond medical knowledge, it is the connection, empathy, and support from healthcare professionals that can truly make a difference in the lives of those living with chronic conditions like diabetes. As with everything, it's the right people.

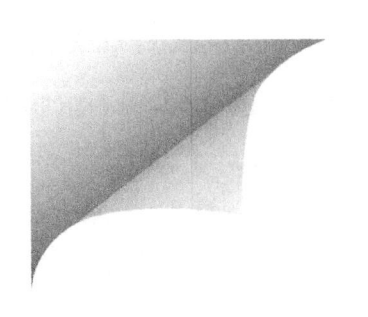

Quote

My secret is no secret. I just do all the things you're supposed to do. I eat right, I sleep, I work out, I'm happy. I choose the good things.

Sharon Stone

Chapter 6

Navigating Life's Rollercoaster: From Loss to Liberation

In February 2017, my father had a massive stroke. It was only two months after he and his twin celebrated their 90th birthday. The birthday celebrations were fantastic. Dad was as proud as punch. He made a speech and was in tip-top form. The stroke came as an awful shock to the family.

I started to feel a huge strain during Dad's time in hospital. I worried about my dad, his care, my mum, and trying to juggle work. I was working on a great project which sometimes meant two to four days away from home. All this took its toll.

In the summer of 2017, Professor O'Shea (by now Dr O' Shea had become a professor) introduced me to the Libre sensor, which was my first experience with technological advancements in diabetes management.

The device contained a reader and a sensor to measure glucose levels without the need for finger-pricking. The sensor is a few centimetres thick and is applied to the skin, usually on the upper arm. Glucose levels can be observed anytime by scanning the reader over the sensor and, even better, using a smartphone App.

I wore the white disc with pride, and it provided great comfort. There was no more finger-pricking and guesswork involved. My numbers would show on my phone and indicate if my blood sugar was going up or down. I was also very excited about the future as I knew that further technology was coming! It made life easier.

In October 2018, 11 months after Dad passed, my Mum passed away too. It was one month before her 90th birthday, and we had planned a big celebration. Truthfully, Mum was just heartbroken and never stopped grieving for Dad. Dad had fought so hard not to die as he wanted to live life to the fullest and Mum wanted to die to be with her love. We were devastated but pleased they were now together.

Bond with a Kindred Spirit – Rachel McDarby

In February 2019, Ray and I decided to go on a ski holiday – our favourite getaway. As we landed at Dublin airport amidst the usual chaos, my eyes landed on this young girl who immediately caught my attention. She had this Libre sensor on her arm, just like mine. It was like an unspoken bond between us, a silent nod that said, "Hey, we're in this together."

She was a stunning blonde with her hair pulled back in a ponytail, rocking a cool outfit and a pair of runners. She had this aura about her as if she were the leader of the pack, the one who made things happen. I couldn't help but see a bit of myself in her – vibrant, confident, and full of life, just like I was twenty years ago.

It turned out her family group was not only on the same flight as us but also staying at the same hotel. What were the odds, right? It felt like having a mini-me around, a kindred spirit in this unexpected encounter. We crossed paths multiple times, exchanging hellos like old friends, connected by this invisible thread that seemed to tie us together.

We introduced ourselves, and subsequently, I found out that Rachels's nickname was Ray, "Ray of Sunshine." Coincidentally, this was also my husband's nickname. Rachel's group of family and friends vanished the first night. Later, I learned they had gone to scatter her mother's ashes on the mountain. Her mother had passed away only three months before, in November, on the same day as my own mother's 90th birthday, another haunting coincidence that tugged at my heart.

On Monday, the group was buzzing in the boot room. The sun was shining, and the conditions were perfect - plenty of snow. We chatted as they got ready to go up the mountain. Later that evening, I spotted them returning. Clearly, they had a great day laughing and joking. I even helped to take off one of the gang's boots. The fun and laughter throughout the hotel were infectious.

On Tuesday morning, in the breakfast room, there was a big happy birthday celebration. A cake arrived for a member of Rachel's group. I looked around and commented to my husband about the fact that Rachel was not present, which I thought was unusual given that she was the life and soul of the group. Before we headed out of the breakfast room, I thought to myself, I hope she is OK.

As we returned to the bedroom after breakfast, we sensed something was seriously wrong in the hotel. The air had turned heavy with sorrow. Tears flowed freely, and hearts broke as the news of Rachel's passing spread. Rachel was found lifeless in her bed, a victim of a cruel sugar low that claimed her in her sleep. The shock was palpable, the grief overwhelming.

Watching her loved ones crumble under the weight of shock, I felt a surge of empathy and helplessness wash over me. It was a stark reminder of life's fragility, the cruel irony of losing someone so young and vibrant to a silent killer like diabetes. The pain was raw, the loss unbearable. To think that this family group travelled to spread their mother's ashes and now, were dealing with the horrific shock of losing their beautiful sister, daughter, and friend because of diabetes.

Later that afternoon, standing outside the hotel as her body was carried away, the shock and disbelief that someone so beautiful could be taken so suddenly was beyond comprehension. It was a moment that seared itself into my soul, a reminder of how fleeting life can be and how precious every moment truly is.

Rachel was only 31 when she passed away, hours after "**The Perfect Day**." This emphasised my reality. Younger, fitter and full of an enormous zest for life, Rachel's death made me feel I was only living on borrowed time.

Later, I learnt that Rachel and her family had an amazing day on the slopes hours before she passed away. The ski conditions had been perfect, and they had a fabulous day, which compounded their shock.

In the months that followed, grief consumed me, tears flowing like a river that never seemed to dry up. Fear gripped me, haunted my nights and casted a shadow over my days. The once comforting presence of the Libre sensor now felt like a fragile shield against the harsh reality of loss and mortality. I never wanted to close my eyes and go to sleep again!

Seeking solace in the wisdom of Professor O'Shea, I embarked on a journey of healing and self-discovery. Through his gentle guidance, he suggested trauma counselling, and this offered a glimmer of hope in the darkness. A lifeline to navigate the storm of emotions that threatened to overwhelm me.

With the aid of my husband's practical guidance, I gradually came to terms with how terrified I felt, and I found the strength to reclaim control of my life, embrace the gift of second chances and live each day with renewed purpose and gratitude.

At this time, Professor O'Shea introduced me to two breakthroughs in diabetes.

The first was the G6Medisense, a blood sugar monitor worn on the body and connected to my smartphone. The significance of this is that the alarm would sound if my blood glucose level went up or down. This meant that at night, I could sleep in the comfort of knowing that if my sugars dipped, an alarm would wake me and I could act accordingly.

This device was hugely comforting to me. I could not help but wonder if Rachel had this device; her outcome may have been different.

The second breakthrough was Victoza, a new drug for treating diabetes. It is a GLP-1 analogue medication that increases incretins, a hormone that helps the body produce more insulin when needed. It also suppresses the amount of glucose produced by the liver. In layman's terms, it helped eliminate the extreme highs and lows.
This was another game-changer.

I now had greater confidence that I could gain control of my diabetes with the G6 Medisense and the Victoza.

Every night, the alarm would go off at least once or twice. The highs and lows were persistent. While my overall HbA1c levels were OK, my day-to-day control was poor. Nighttime was a real challenge. Truthfully, I was happy running my sugars high, and it became my personal private coping strategy to avoid the dreaded nighttime sugar lows.

Three months later, on 20th May 2019, my eldest brother Adrian, passed away from cancer. Adrian was also my godfather, my mentor, and my confidant. I was bereft and broken.

I just felt like I was being repeatedly punched. I felt lost and terrified. The loss of three close family members and Rachel's cruel demise left me wondering how I was going to get beyond this. All the tools and strategies I had learnt had just vanished, and I had no idea how to get back on track.

Christmas arrived, and we thought, "Let's go skiing again!" We decided to have a Christmas getaway and have some fun, which we did. We went to a different country and resort.

We returned from skiing in early January 2020. In February, I was admitted to hospital with cellulitis on my face and eye. A simple stye had quickly developed into this horrific infection because my body's immune system had weakened completely. I could not combat an infection. The cellulitis endangered my sight due to its proximity to my eye. My body was severely depleted from the cumulative toll of my experiences. Neglecting self-care, my blood sugar levels spiralled out of control, resulting in essential medical intervention.

Alone in my hospital room, I dreaded the nighttime as I was so afraid of having a sugar low that would render me helpless to deal with my condition. I hadn't realised how terrified of being alone with my diabetes, even in a hospital, was gripping me.

In March 2020, COVID-19 hit Europe, and a new fear engulfed me. Every day on the news, reporters would discuss high-risk, vulnerable people, and that list included people with diabetes. I realised lockdown suited me. I worked from home, rested when I needed to, and generally lived a very healthy life in my giant bubble with my husband.

In May 2020, Ray started to show symptoms that he was unwell. We were deep in the throes of lockdown, which made it difficult to receive medical care. Five months later, Ray was diagnosed with a brain tumour. Despite the overwhelming stress and fear, my total focus shifted away from myself, my diabetes and the many bereavements and my attention was entirely on Ray's recovery. I kicked into total organisational mode, firing on all cylinders to ensure he got the right care, attention, and support. Ray had been there for me since the moment we met, and now it was my turn to reciprocate and ensure his return to good health.

Ray had surgery in December 2020, and due to COVID-19, he was alone in the hospital, and I was alone at home. Worried about Ray, I revisited my greatest fear. The vicious circle of being alone with my diabetes returned. I was afraid to be asleep and returned to my old friend, "Mr Nighttime Sugar High", my private coping strategy.

Ray showed resilience. His first words after surgery were, "Brilliant, now let's get back to normal and start enjoying life again". His ability to move forward, never look back, never feel sorry for himself enabled him to smash through. It was amazing to watch and learn from him. We really are a great team together!

On top of this came menopause, which brought a whole new level of nighttime horrors. Hormones clashed like waves on rocks in a storm every night; I was awakened by alarms several times a night. Daytime was a right off. I no longer had the energy to work or the interest in doing anything. I genuinely felt dead from the inside out.

I realised it was time to get help. I knew I couldn't keep going like this. Ray was now fit and healthy, and we had a bright future ahead of us. I had to get some help and take action. I knew I didn't want to live my life in continuous fear. I was once an extremely confident girl who loved life, loved to party, and loved to say yes to anything. I had to find myself. The girl without the fear.

I met with Professor O'Shea in 2022, and together, we analysed my symptoms and my options. Ultimately, we decided I should switch to the insulin pump. While the pump was not a new device it had benefitted from developing technology.

Quote

Chasing perfection with type-I diabetes is impossible. There's so much that's out of your hands and finding a way to remain calm and patient in moments where diabetes interrupts your life is the key.

Nick Jonas

Chapter 7

The T Slim Pump - How AI Helped Change My Life

In May 2023, I was super excited to receive my new T Slim Pump. A few days later, I attended the hospital for T Slim training. I was absolutely thrilled, but I was also nervous, mainly because I was unsure if I would understand the system. What does it do? How does it work? I had dreamt of the positive effects this would have on my life and desperately wanted it to be successful.

The insulin pump is a device—known as a hybrid closed-loop system—that uses a high-tech algorithm to determine the amount of insulin needed to keep the wearer's blood sugar levels steady and delivers the required insulin via a pump.

Control-IQ technology automatically adjusts insulin levels based on the Dexcom G6 CGM readings.

The system uses a predictive algorithm to minimise wide fluctuations in glucose, increasing my time in range. It delivers insulin every 5 minutes and can even predict glucose levels 30 minutes in advance. It adjusts insulin delivery accordingly, including automatic correction boluses. In a nutshell, it keeps my blood sugars in range 95% of the time.

The training was simple, and the representative gave me a comprehensive user guide. My diabetes nurse was also involved, and together, we worked out what I needed based on the insulin I was consistently injecting and used this to program the pump. This was calculated based on the fact that I was injecting slow-release insulin twice a day and fast-acting insulin every time I ate. In the old world, I had been injecting myself 5 to 6 times daily.

As I was leaving with my fantastic new pump attached to me like a baby, I was super excited and nervous. This was a big step in starting to trust something alien to me for my survival, but I was ready for new beginnings.

That night, Ray and I went to bed with my new baby propped in between us, attached to me like an umbilical cord. I went to sleep, and at about 3am, Ray woke me.

"Lorraine, I think the machine is broken; you have a flat line going all the way across, and there are no alarms."

I leapt out of the bed – flatlining? Holy crap, I was dying!

I decided to get the old-style finger prick machine out of the drawer and check my blood sugar. Unbelievably, my blood sugars were perfectly within range. We both agreed to try to go back to sleep and address the situation in the morning.

The next morning, the machine still showed a perfect, steady, straight line. No alarms, no sugar low, no sugar highs - just perfection.
We thought it must have been a fluke, a one-off. Sceptical, we decided to wait and see what the rest of the day and night would bring.

The following night, the same thing happened: I flatlined! There were no alarms, no sugar highs, no lows. For the first time in 28 years, I was not awakened because of my blood sugars. I did not sweat, need Lucozade, fear, or gulp to survive.

This was life-changing, and I was so blessed to have my T Slim Pump.

Within one week of using this new technology, I became obsessed. I could never imagine life without this pump, and I hope I never have to. For the first time, I have an uninterrupted night's sleep. But most significant for me was that my fear had been swapped to contentment.

From the moment I laid my hands on the T Slim insulin pump, my life took an extraordinary turn. Gone were the days of erratic sugar highs and debilitating lows. The consistent control it offered was nothing short of miraculous. I now had the positive reassurance that I had longed for.

As each week passed, I found myself filled with a newfound sense of confidence. The device became more than just a piece of technology; it became a companion on my journey to better health. With each successful adjustment and precise dose, my worries and anxieties began to fade away. I programmed it for everything I did, from short weekly walks to long weekend hikes, ski trips, and weekend socialising.

The impact of the T Slim insulin pump transcended beyond just my blood sugar levels. I noticed a remarkable transformation in my overall well-being.

I felt fitter and healthier, an energy that I had forgotten I possessed. The pump was not just a tool for managing my diabetes but a catalyst for a more vibrant and fulfilling life.

I have tested my insulin pump in various scenarios, from lazy Sundays to adventurous holidays and even exhilarating ski trips. Each experience has tested my pump's reliability and my ability to manage my diabetes in various settings.

The changes were so profound that I felt compelled to share my experience with the world. I wanted to shout from the rooftops about the remarkable difference the T Slim insulin pump had made in my life. It was not just a device; it was a beacon of hope and empowerment.

With each passing day, I found myself eager to introduce my pump to everyone I met. Its impact was not just personal but a testament to the transformative power of innovation and technology in managing diabetes. The T Slim insulin pump had not just changed my life; it had become a part of who I was, propelling me towards a brighter and healthier future.

I started my pump journey in May 2023, and after six months, I visited Professor O'Shea. I had my bloods taken ahead of my appointment, and I could also download and send every daily recording from my insulin pump. Professor O'Shea, Trisha, the diabetic nurse, and I were just blown away by the transformation. Once again, I was crying with him, but they were tears of total joy, relief and happiness.

Every blood result showed incredible improvements. Professor O'Shea was delighted that we had finally got there. During the twenty-three years of my journey with him, we had only dreamt of gaining almost perfect control, perfect HbA1c, and perfect blood sugar all around.
I skipped out of that meeting, the wind in my face, confident that life had just got a whole lot better. I was so excited.

My life had been a whirlwind of roller coasters, filled with deep emotions of sadness, fear, and heartache. However, amidst the chaos, my story is ultimately about hope. It's about never giving up, no matter what lemon life throws at me.

Together with my husband Ray, Professor O'Shea, and his team, we embraced the power of teamwork. We had tirelessly worked towards new approaches, constantly striving for solutions. Trust has been the foundation of our journey, as we trusted each other's intuition. Even though there had been many failed attempts, we never gave up. Perseverance was our mantra, pushing us through the tough times. Each experience brought growth and made me stronger and wiser. I am so grateful for the unwavering support, love, and commitment from all those involved in my journey.

Resilience has been my armour. It has helped me bounce back from adversity and fuel my search for the right answers.
I have decided to share my story in the hope of inspiring and uplifting others who may be facing their own challenges in life—no matter what those roller coasters may be, but especially if they are health-related.

If you have a friend, sister, or brother with diabetes, or if you are a parent of someone who has diabetes, I hope that my personal story helps you understand the challenges and how the technological landscape is changing daily to help manage this condition.

A Pump of Hope

My Management and Control Before and After the Pump

Diabetes represents a major public health concern, and efforts to control hyperglycemia are an essential element of the management of patients with type 1 diabetes.

Hyperglycemia is measured using a haemoglobin A1c (HbA1c) test, which assesses the average blood glucose level in the preceding 60–120 days.

For diabetes patients, an HbA1c target of 6.5% (48 mmol/mol) is recommended because it lowers the risk of developing diabetic complications. I presented myself to the clinic for many years with high HbA1cs of over 10%. I was in the high-risk category for cardiovascular disease. There is a strong relationship between high HbA1c readings and the risk of developing diabetes-related complications.

I was permanently exhausted. I would pull myself out of bed in the morning, drag myself around and have zero zest or energy for life. For someone who loved socialising, I dreaded an invite and wondered how I would escape and get home to bed. Sometimes, depending on how high my blood sugar was, I could end up in the emergency room with severe hypoglycemia.

High blood sugar levels can cause blindness, poor vision, and other common eye diseases. Like the eyes, heart, and nervous system, high blood glucose levels can damage blood vessels in the kidneys, and for many years, I was at high risk for these diseases.

Within three months of wearing the pump, my HbA1c went from 10% to 6%. This meant that within three months, I had dropped from being in a high-risk category for so many other complications to now being in the fit and healthy category.

I no longer need to visit my GP regularly. Previously, a common cold would turn nasty quickly; the slightest bang on my toe, a cut on my finger, or a stye in my eye would mean several courses of antibiotics or hospitalisation. My ability to fight any infection was low, and my immune system was severely challenged.

But since starting the pump, my GP thought I had moved to another clinic as he had not seen me in months.

Technology has moved so fast. Originally, I would carry a handbag-sized blood glucose monitor to finger prick, place a droplet of blood onto a stick, and wait 90 seconds for a blood reading. My fingertips became painful and hardened because I had to do this up to 15 times a day.

I was thrilled when I received my first continuous blood glucose monitor, the Libre Sensor, for my arm. It felt great to zap my phone against the Libre to read my blood sugars. Moving from finger pricking to this made such a difference to my life.

The next game-changer for me was calculating how much insulin I needed to take. I mentioned previously that I had attended the DAFNE course. This taught me how to count carbs; for every 10 grams of carbs I had, I would take a ratio of insulin. Every 10 grams was counted as 1 carb. It sounded easy, but there was a huge amount of guesswork at the beginning.

For example, if I were to take a slice of bread and guessed it to be about 20 grams of carbs, and I had a ratio of 1:1, meaning for every 1 gram of carb I consumed, I had to take 1 unit of insulin, then I would calculate 2 units of insulin for the bread.

However, this was complicated depending on the time of the day, I had different insulin sensitivity. For example, in the mornings, I needed a 2:1 ratio. Again, this means that for every unit of carb I consumed, I needed to take 2 units of insulin, so now that bread would need 4 units, but in the evening, I may drop to half a unit of insulin. Any mistake would have a knock-on effect, like a sugar low in the middle of the night.

Then when night came, I would panic when having a sugar low; I would overcompensate for the low and pour a jug of milk into the box of cornflakes and eat the whole lot. This resulted in a very high swing of increased blood sugar in the morning.

The pump removes the need for all of this; it eliminates all the guesswork, the ratio calculations, and swings of highs and lows - All gone!

Not only have I reduced my blood sugars, but I have also reduced my anxiety about not having calculated my insulin correctly. When I was at a restaurant, I would often text Ray and ask him if I had calculated my insulin dosage correctly. I now never need to do this. AI does it!

At night, I can sleep, knowing that even if I go low, the machine will catch it and stop me from going into a deep low. And even if I do have a sugar low, the alarms go off, and I would take a sip of the measured glucose drink beside my bed.

To say that I feel like I have won the lotto is an understatement. I am now brimming with energy, fit, healthy, and steady.

Quote

Don't let yourself fall, you gotta pick yourself right up and strive to do better and be better! Think positive. Don't let the Diabetes control you! You control the Diabetes! Be strong because someways might be tough but you are tougher!

Tiffany Danczak

Chapter 8

Empowered Living: Navigating the Three Pillars of Control

In the culmination of my journey, I reflect on the pivotal moment when I first encountered Professor O'Shea and learned the fundamental equation that would become the cornerstone of my success: Food + Insulin + Emotion = Great Control. This simple yet profound formula encapsulated the interconnectedness of what we consume, how our bodies respond to insulin, and the impact of our emotions on our overall health.

Armed with this revelation, I embarked on a transformative path to conquer these three pillars and attain the level of control I desired. Each component played a vital role in shaping my health and quality of life, and understanding their interplay became the key to unlocking a new level of well-being.

As I delved deeper into this journey, I encountered challenges and breakthroughs that tested my resolve and pushed me to explore new ways of managing my health.

Diabetes is one of the only diseases that YOU actually control. Yes, it's controlled by insulin, but that's only a part of it. It's controlled by YOU adjusting insulin, by YOU exercising, by YOUR decisions about what food to eat and how much sleep you need. And, of course, you are supported by a medical team, but it's ultimately up to you to gain control. In my case, if I am lucky, I get to see my endocrinologist team twice a year, as these clinics are so busy, I'm lucky to get 15 minutes at a time. This means a total of 30 minutes per year! It's impossible to learn and get all your answers in that short space of time. So, exploring and understanding what has a positive and negative impact on your sugar level is critical. Remember that everyone is different, and your journey is unique to you.

My decision to embrace AI was a massive turning point. It helped an important element of the equation: Automatically delivering the required level of insulin.

Through the subsequent chapters, I have shared the tools and techniques that have become invaluable allies in my quest for control. From practical meal planning strategies to nuanced insights on emotional well-being, each lesson learned has empowered me to make informed decisions aligned with my goals.

As I conclude this book, I sincerely hope that the wisdom imparted within these pages will guide others in navigating their own paths. May the tools shared inspire and empower you, offering solace and strength in moments of uncertainty. May you embrace the journey towards greater control with resilience and determination, knowing that you possess the power to overcome any obstacle that stands in your way.

In the end, remember this: empowerment lies not only in mastering external factors but also in unwavering belief in your ability to thrive despite the challenges that may arise. May you embrace this truth and embark on your own journey towards empowered living, armed with the knowledge that you are capable of achieving greatness.

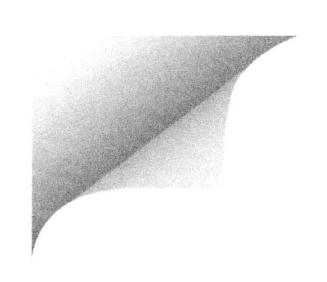

> # Quote
>
> Every day is an absolute battle. I don't care what anyone says. You have to wake up and say to yourself, 'I accept that I have diabetes, and I'm not going to let it run my entire life.
>
> Bret Michaels

PART TWO

Tips For Making Your Life Easier While Living With Diabetes.

Food + Insulin + Emotion = Good Control

As I mentioned, Professor O'Shea always said that there were three main components to my good diabetes control.

The following chapters offer some practical hints and tips that I've learned over the years to help with all three components. I've often struggled with which one to start with first because, for me, they are all equally important. It's a bit like a wheel; if one part is out of sync, it will impact the other parts.

Chapter 9

Sleep

Sleep is vital to my life as someone living with diabetes. The impact of a night's rest on my well-being and blood sugar levels is profound, shaping my ability to navigate each day with stability and vitality. When I experience a terrible night's sleep, the repercussions linger for days, affecting my energy, mood, and overall productivity.

Picture this: after an uninterrupted and peaceful 8-hour sleep, I wake up feeling rejuvenated and full of energy. My blood sugar levels are stable, and my mood is lifted. I can conquer anything that comes my way. I exercise, set goals, and manifest positivity throughout the day, undeterred by challenges.

On the flip side, a night of poor sleep can set off a chain reaction of events that impact my diabetes management and well-being. Imagine this scenario: as I prepare to drift off to sleep, I come across engaging content on social media. Whether it's a tempting dress, an exciting movie, or a discussion with Ray about a holiday, these stimuli trigger a surge of emotions that disrupt my ability to fall asleep peacefully.

The emotional energy consumed by these distractions can lead to fluctuations in my blood sugar levels during the night, potentially resulting in a dip around 3 am. Waking up feeling exhausted and drained, I find it challenging to muster the energy to exercise, concentrate, or complete simple tasks. The fatigue and anxiety linger throughout the day, making it difficult to regain my momentum until I can achieve a restful night's sleep again.

I have established specific guidelines that work for me to address these challenges and prioritise my sleep.

- I avoid drinking fluids an hour before bedtime. It prevents me from waking up at 3 a.m. needing the loo as I will be awake for the rest of the night.
- I keep distractions like TV out of the bedroom, a habit that inadvertently improved my quality of rest. This wasn't a conscious decision I made; it purely happened by accident. Our TV broke in the room, and after a few weeks of not replacing it, I noticed how much calmer the room was and as a result, I now have no TV in the room. (Much to my husband's horror).
- I avoid social media before bed, as scrolling has been linked to poor sleep and blood sugar management.
- I wear an eye mask to completely block out light.

- All significant discussions are held outside the bedroom. For example, If Ray asked me where we would like to go on holiday, that would prompt a real inner excitement. He would then head off to sleep, and I would be left with a whizzing head. Which, in turn, will cause a low sugar level. A simple question like, did you pay the gas bill, will cause me anxiety.
- Sometimes, I would try to do even 10 minutes of Yoga before bed.
- I do some journaling, especially Gratification.

The connection between sleep and diabetes management is deeply personal to me and has a huge impact on my emotional state. Each night's rest, or lack thereof, has a tangible impact on my blood sugar control, mood, and daily experiences. By acknowledging the importance of quality sleep and tailoring my routine to prioritise rest, I strive to optimise my diabetes management and overall quality of life.

> "I made a lot of mistakes trying to juggle this condition with my career, and I think that's a pretty common experience for type I diabetics. This can be a very isolating condition, one that makes you feel hopeless sometimes."
>
> Alexandra Park- Actress

Chapter 10

Manifesting, Gratitude & all Things Roxie Nafousi

I have always tried to be a positive person. Many moons ago, I read and listened to "The Secret" and used to journal with it. During my corporate life, planning and goal setting were my main focus. I wrote everything down and maintained a clear mindset.

However, life has thrown so much at me that I genuinely couldn't see the wood from the trees, and fear had taken over everything, paralysing me.

I started following a manifesting queen on Instagram and liked her. I found her to be genuine, and she delivered simple tools and techniques. I was delighted when she brought out a book called "Manifest," and I began to purchase all the merchandise associated with it. I was very fortunate to see her in Dublin when she visited. My friend Mary and I went to see her. Mary was very ill with an incurable cancer, and the day gave us peace and hope and provided a joyous time together.

Since then, I have practised Gratitude every day. Life can get overwhelming, and it impacts my sugars so quickly.

Gratitude helps you see the blessings in life and all the positives. It helps you not feel sorry for yourself. It empowers and reminds you that you've got this!

Here is a list of what I would be very grateful for, and yes, I write them down every night. Over and over again. I have a gratitude journal that captures my daily thoughts.

- I am grateful I woke up today feeling fit & healthy
- I am grateful for steady blood sugars
- I am grateful for the T Slim pump I wear
- I am grateful for the medical team I have and the constant support they give me
- I am so thankful for Dr O'Shea
- I am grateful for Ray, our relationship and how happy I am
- I am grateful for the friends and family I have around me and for the support I receive
- I am thankful for the moments of peace and relaxation that contribute to my mental and emotional health

- I am a warrior - I got this
- I am so grateful that Jackie, Mum, Dad & Adrian are watching over me and guiding me along my way

Use the space provided on the following pages to create your own list of gratitude that you wish to repeat daily.

Here are a few of my favourite gurus that I follow:

1. Roxi Nafousi – My bible ! I love it and try to live by it.

2. Gabby Bernstein

3. Steve Bartlett

DAILY GRATITUDE

List Of Things That I am Grateful For

Date:

-
-
-
-
-
-
-
-
-
-
-
-
-

DAILY GRATITUDE

List Of Things That I am Grateful For

Date: _____

-

-

-

-

-

-

-

-

-

-

-

-

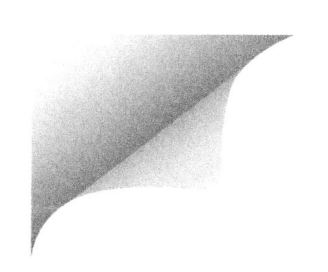

Quote

My diabetes is such a central part of my life... It did teach me discipline... it also taught me about moderation... I've trained myself to be super-vigilant... because I feel better when I am in control.

Sonia Sotomayor

Chapter 11

Exercise

As someone living with type 1 diabetes, I understand the importance of maintaining a healthy lifestyle. I think that over the years, I have tried every exercise imaginable.

I joined a cricket team one summer. We had such fun over the summer, and I was super proud to have won a medal for the county. However, the sport did not love me. I felt that all the running would greatly impact my sugar. I would have to stack up on glucose in order to go to the game, and given that the game can last up to 3 or 4 hours when I come home, I would inevitably have a sugar low late in the evening.

Jill, my pal, convinced me to join 'The Couch to 5K' challenge. Again, I loved the group and the exercise. I think it was more about being outdoors, which I loved so much, and I suppose also my competitiveness. However, running did not suit me, so I parked it after I achieved the goal.

I started incorporating strength-training exercises into my workout routine, and I was amazed by the positive impact it had on my blood sugar levels. Not only did I notice improved insulin sensitivity, but I also experienced more stable blood glucose readings throughout the day.

Over time, I began to feel stronger and more energised, and I noticed that my overall well-being had significantly improved. Combining strength-building exercises and regular cardiovascular activity helped me better manage my diabetes and maintain a healthier lifestyle.

I now have a personal trainer, which my husband and I attend together. We do this three mornings a week, and it's only for 30 minutes. But those thirty minutes are the most important sessions for me in the week. We now love them so much for our overall well-being and would rarely miss them.

They are not just good for insulin and diabetes; they are amazing for my health and mind.

Walking is the cardio that most suits me. During COVID, it was an opportunity to meet with pals, and we have continued with this habit even to this day. Every Sunday, we walk to a lighthouse approximately 20 kilometres away. I put my T Slim into exercise mode, and I have no issues. There are no spikes, no lows, and it's fantastic.

Through this journey, I learned that strength-building exercises not only contribute to physical strength but also plays a crucial role in managing type 1 diabetes. I'm grateful for discovering this valuable addition to my diabetes management plan, and I'm committed to continuing this beneficial practice for years to come.

For me, even if it's only 15 minutes of walking every day, you will never regret it, and your body will be so grateful for it.

Then, on a yearly basis, we love to Ski. I am not the most confident, and at times, due to my sugars not being stable, I would have high anxiety. But this year, with the pump, I was much more confident.

The pump has made a huge difference to my training and being stable 90% of the time and being in the sugar range 95% of the time has made such a difference.

Here are some more activities I have tried and love to incorporate into my monthly routine and are generally considered suitable for individuals with type 1 diabetes as they help build strength without significantly impacting blood sugars:

Find one that you love because consistency is key. Doing something on repeat daily, weekly, and monthly will help control. Remember, what you did yesterday will impact today.

1. Resistance Training:
- *Weightlifting:* Strength training exercises using free weights, resistance bands, or weight machines can help build muscle strength and improve overall fitness. Start with light weights and gradually increase the intensity as your strength improves.
- *Bodyweight Exercises:* Exercises like push-ups, squats, lunges, and planks can be practical for building strength and muscle tone without needing equipment.

There are recognised benefits of strength training for those approaching menopause.

2. Walking:

Brisk walking is probably my favourite exercise, and it certainly got us through the lockdown. It's a simple yet effective exercise for building strength, improving cardiovascular health, and managing blood sugar levels. Incorporate walking into your daily routine or add interval training to increase intensity.

Even 20 minutes every day makes such a difference. Pick a point, walk to it, and back again. There is no need to do marathons.

3. Yoga:

Yoga poses and stretches can improve flexibility, balance, and strength while promoting relaxation and stress reduction. Yoga can be a gentle yet effective way to build strength and improve overall well-being. I go on YouTube and find free sessions. I do one or two sessions a week, especially before bedtime. It helps relax me and clears my mind.

Yoga poses and stretches can improve flexibility, balance, and strength while promoting relaxation and stress reduction. Yoga can be a gentle yet effective way to build strength and improve overall well-being. I go on YouTube and find free sessions. I do one or two sessions a week, especially before bedtime. It helps my mind.

4. Pilates:

Pilates focuses on core strength, flexibility, and body alignment through controlled movements and exercises. It can help improve muscle tone, posture, and overall strength without causing significant fluctuations in blood sugar levels.

5. Swimming:

Swimming is a low-impact aerobic exercise that also helps build muscle strength. It provides a full-body workout, improves cardiovascular fitness, and is gentle on the joints, making it an excellent option for individuals with type 1 diabetes. I was also one of those beginner swimmers, but truthfully, I am more about bobbing around in the water. Again, it's great for the mind.

6. Cycling:

Cycling outdoors or on a stationary bike is a cardiovascular exercise that can also help build leg strength. It is a low-impact activity that can be easily adjusted for intensity and duration to suit individual fitness levels. I love to cycle in and around our village at any opportunity, especially in mild weather.

Monitoring blood sugar levels before, during, and after exercise is essential to understanding how different activities affect your body. Based on your exercise routine and individual response, consider adjusting your carbohydrate intake, and insulin dosage and monitoring frequency.

Quote

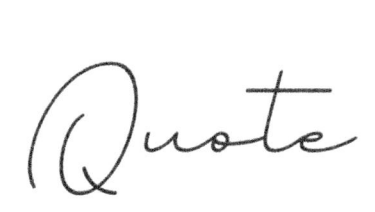

I just took the chance. [Diabetes] wasn't going to stop me from playing. There was no fear. I was never convinced that anything would keep me from getting back to playing.

Austin Freeman

Chapter 12

Food

Here are the Top 10 tips for healthy eating as outlined by the Diabetes.org.Uk

What does eating right mean for you?

If you have type 1 diabetes, it is crucial to monitor your carb intake to maintain stable blood glucose levels. This involves estimating the number of carbs in your meal and matching it with the appropriate amount of insulin needed.

Whether you have type 1 or type 2 diabetes, it is important to make healthier food choices if you need to lose, gain, or maintain your weight.

Considering your portion sizes is also important, regardless of your diabetes type. This makes it easier to calculate nutritional information when carb counting or managing your weight. Keep in mind that portion sizes vary for each person, so what works for someone else may not be suitable for you.

If you feel overwhelmed about your feelings about food and diabetes, we have plenty of information to help you.

1. Choose healthier carbohydrates

All carbs affect blood glucose levels so it's important to know which foods contain carbohydrates. Choose the healthier foods that contain carbs and be aware of your portion sizes.

Here are some healthy sources of carbohydrate:

- whole grains like brown rice, buckwheat and whole oats
- fruit
- vegetables
- pulses such as chickpeas, beans and lentils
- Unsweetened yoghurt and milk.

At the same time, it's also important to cut down on foods low in fibre such as white bread, white rice and highly-processed cereals. You can check food labels when you're looking for foods high in fibre if you're unsure.

2. Eat less salt

Diabetes sufferers are at a greater risk of high blood pressure which increases the chance of heart disease and stroke. It is vitally important to reduce salt intake to minimise these health problems.

Try to limit yourself to a maximum of 6g (one teaspoonful) of salt a day. Lots of pre-packaged foods already contain salt so remember to check food labels and choose those with less salt. Cooking from scratch will help you keep an eye on how much salt you're eating. You can also get creative and swap out salt for different types of herbs and spices to add that extra flavour.

3. Eat less red and processed meat

If you're cutting down on carbs, you might start to have bigger portions of meat to fill you up. But it's not a good idea to do this with red and processed meat, for example ham, bacon, sausages, beef and lamb. These all have links with heart problems and cancers.

Try swapping red and processed meat for these:

- pulses such as beans and lentils
- eggs
- fish
- poultry for example chicken and turkey
- unsalted nuts

Beans, peas and lentils are also very high in fibre and don't affect your blood glucose levels too much – making them a great swap for processed and red meat and keeping you feeling full. Most of us know that fish is good for us, but oily fish like salmon and mackerel are even better.

These are rich in something called omega-3 oil, which helps protect your heart. Try and aim to eat two portions of oily fish a week.

4. Eat more fruit and veg

We know eating fruit and veg is good for you. It's always a good thing to aim to eat more at mealtimes and have them as snacks if you're hungry. This can help you get the vitamins, minerals and fibre your body needs every day to help keep you healthy.

You might be wondering about fruit and if you should avoid it because it's sugary? The answer is no. Whole fruit is good for everyone and if you have diabetes, it's no different. Fruits do contain sugar, but it's natural sugar. This is different to the added sugar (also known as free sugars) that are in things like chocolate, biscuits and cakes.

Products like fruit juices also count as added sugar, so go for whole fruit instead. This can be fresh, frozen, dried or tinned (in juice, not in syrup). And it's best to eat it throughout the day instead of one bigger portion in one go.

5. Choose healthier fats

We all need fat in our diet because it gives us energy. But different types of fat affect our health in different ways.

Healthier fats are in foods like unsalted nuts, seeds, avocados, oily fish, olive oil, rapeseed oil and sunflower oil. Some saturated fats can increase the amount of cholesterol in your blood, increasing your risk of heart problems. These are mainly found in animal products and prepared food like:

- red and processed meat
- ghee
- butter
- lard
- biscuits, cakes, pies and pastries.

It's still a good idea to cut down on using oils in general, so try to grill, steam or bake foods instead.

6. Cut down on free sugar

We know cutting out sugar can be really hard at the beginning, so small practical swaps are a good starting point when you're trying to cut down on excess sugar. Swapping sugary drinks, energy drinks and fruit juices with water, plain milk, or tea and coffee without sugar can be a good start.

Cutting out free sugars can help you manage your blood glucose levels and help you manage your weight. You can always try low or zero-calorie sweeteners (also known as artificial or non-sugar sweeteners) to help you cut back. These can also be helpful for weight loss in the short term if you don't swap for other foods and drinks containing lots of calories. But, in the long term, try and reduce the overall sweetness in your diet.

7. Be smart with snacks

If you want a snack, choose yoghurts, unsalted nuts, seeds, fruits and vegetables instead of crisps, chips, biscuits and chocolates. Always pay attention to your portion size as this will aid weight control.

8. Drink alcohol sensibly

Alcohol is high in calories, so if you do drink and you're trying to lose weight, think about cutting back. Try to keep to a maximum of 14 units a week. But spread it out to avoid binge drinking, and go several days a week without alcohol.

If you take insulin or other diabetes medications, it's also not a good idea to drink on an empty stomach. This is because alcohol can make hypos more likely to happen.

9. Don't bother with so-called diabetic food

To say food is a "diabetic food" is now against the law. This is because there isn't any evidence that these foods offer you a special benefit over eating healthily. They can also often contain just as much fat and calories as similar products, and can still affect your blood glucose level. These foods can also sometimes have a laxative effect.

10. Get your minerals and vitamins from foods

There's no evidence that mineral and vitamin supplements help you manage your diabetes. So, unless you've been told to take something by your healthcare team, like folic acid for pregnancy, you don't need to take supplements.

It's better to get your essential nutrients by eating a mixture of different foods. This is because some supplements can affect your medications or make some diabetes complications worse, like kidney disease.

11. Don't forget to keep moving

Being more physically active goes hand in hand with eating healthier. It can help you manage your diabetes and also reduce your risk of heart problems. This is because it increases the amount of glucose used by your muscles and helps the body use insulin more efficiently.

Try to aim for at least 150 minutes of moderate-intensity activity a week. This is any activity that raises your heart rate, makes you breathe faster and feel warmer. You should still be able to talk and only be slightly out of breath. And you don't have to do all 150 minutes in one go. Break it down into bite-size chunks of 10 minutes throughout the week or 30 minutes 5 times a week.

Using the T Slim Pump

One remarkable benefit of using an insulin pump is its newfound flexibility regarding food choices and meal timing. Unlike in the past, when skipping a meal could have serious consequences, now, with the Pump, it is possible to forgo a meal if necessary.

While this is not recommended, there are times when it may happen. I find myself only eating two meals a day now. I may choose to have breakfast and dinner or opt for lunch and dinner instead. Having this level of control over my eating schedule is genuinely empowering.

Adjusting my meals according to my lifestyle and preferences has been a game-changer. It allows me to manage my blood sugar levels better and ensures I can enjoy my meals without worrying about the timing. This flexibility has also made navigating social events and unexpected changes in my daily routine easier.

In addition to the convenience of meal planning, the insulin pump has also helped me develop a more intuitive approach to eating. I have learned to listen to my body's hunger cues and adjust my meals accordingly. This has not only improved my overall eating habits but has also contributed to better blood sugar control.

Overall, the flexibility that the insulin pump provides regarding food has dramatically enhanced my quality of life. It has given me the freedom to enjoy my meals on my terms and empowered me to take control of my diabetes management in a way that works best for me.

Overall, meal planning is a proactive approach to diabetes management that empowers individuals to make informed food choices, control blood sugar levels, and support overall well-being. It serves as a tool for achieving stable blood sugar control, maintaining a healthy lifestyle, and optimising diabetes management.

Suggested Breakfasts

On the following pages, there are 10 of my top 'go-to' breakfast ideas.

Note: I don't count GI index - I use the foundations of DAFNE, which I learned back in 2017, carb counting.

Creating low-impact breakfast suggestions for individuals wearing an insulin pump involves considering foods' glycaemic index (GI). The GI measures how quickly a food raises blood sugar levels. Foods with a low GI are digested and absorbed more slowly, leading to a steadier rise in blood sugar levels. Here are ten breakfast suggestions with low to moderate GI to help minimise the impact on blood sugar levels:

These suggestions provide a balance of carbohydrates, proteins, fats, and fibre to help manage blood sugar levels when wearing an insulin pump. Monitoring individual responses to these breakfast options and adjusting insulin dosage accordingly is essential.

Breakfast Ideas

1. Oatmeal with nuts and seeds:

Oatmeal has a low to medium GI, and adding nuts and seeds provides healthy fats and proteins that can further reduce the GI impact.

2. Greek yogurt with berries:

Greek yogurt has a lower GI than regular yogurt, and the addition of berries adds fibre and natural sweetness with a relatively low GI.

3. Scrambled eggs with spinach and whole-grain toast:

Eggs have a GI of 0, and pairing them with fibre-rich spinach and whole-grain toast helps slow down the release of glucose into the bloodstream.

4. Smoothie with spinach, avocado, and protein powder:

Adding leafy greens and healthy fats like avocado to a smoothie can help lower its overall GI, and protein powder provides a sustained release of energy.

5. Chia seed pudding:

Chia seeds have a very low GI and are high in fibre, making chia seed pudding a great low-impact breakfast option.

Breakfast Ideas

6 Cottage Cheese with Sliced Peaches:

Cottage cheese has a low GI, and pairing it with fibre-rich peaches can help maintain steady blood sugar levels.

7 Veggie omelette with whole grain toast:

Including various vegetables in an omelette provides fibre, vitamins, and minerals, while entire grain toast adds complex carbohydrates with a moderate GI.

8 Quinoa breakfast bowl with nuts and fruit:

Quinoa has a moderate GI and is rich in protein and fibre. Adding nuts and fruit further enhances its nutritional value without significantly impacting blood sugar levels.

9 Smoked salmon on rye bread:

Smoked salmon is a good source of protein and healthy fats, while rye bread has a lower GI than white bread.

10 Low-sugar, high-fibre cereal with almond milk:

Choose a high-fibre cereal with minimal added sugars and pair it with unsweetened almond milk for a low-impact breakfast option.

Meal Planning

Meal planning is a crucial aspect of managing diabetes. As we know, food is a vital part of diabetes control, and too often, I roll into a Monday not having food in the house or grabbing something "handy", and the impact that it has on my sugars could have a ripple effect for the next 24 hours.

1. Blood Sugar Control: Meal planning helps regulate blood sugar levels by consistently consuming carbohydrates, proteins, and fats throughout the day. This helps prevent spikes and dips in blood sugar levels, promoting better diabetes control.

2. Carb Counting: Planning meals in advance allows individuals with diabetes to calculate and distribute carbohydrate intake evenly across meals and snacks. This helps match insulin doses to carbohydrate intake, leading to more accurate blood sugar management.

3. Nutrient Balance: A well-planned meal balances nutrients, including carbohydrates, proteins, fats, vitamins, and minerals. This balance is essential for overall health, energy levels, and optimal body functioning, especially for individuals with diabetes.

4. Weight Management: Meal planning can help achieve and maintain a healthy weight, which is essential for diabetes management. By portioning meals appropriately and making nutritious food choices, individuals can control calorie intake and support weight goals.

5. Consistency and Routine: Establishing a meal plan creates a sense of structure and routine in daily eating habits. Consistency in meal timing and composition can help stabilise blood sugar levels and reduce the risk of fluctuations that may occur with irregular eating patterns.

6. Avoiding Unhealthy Choices: Planning meals in advance allows individuals to make healthier food choices and avoid impulsively selecting high-sugar or high-fat options. This can help prevent sudden spikes in blood sugar levels and promote long-term health.

Alcohol

In discussing the essentials of managing diabetes, it's imperative to recognise that our relationship with food extends beyond mere sustenance; it intertwines with our social fabric, where gatherings often involve the presence of alcohol.

Therefore, any conversation about food and its impact on diabetes would be incomplete without addressing the role of alcohol intake.

Understanding how alcohol interacts with our bodies and our blood sugar levels is vital for maintaining a balanced and healthy lifestyle as a person with diabetes.

My history with alcohol has been a rollercoaster ride. I would have labelled myself as a binge drinker, swinging between extremes of all or nothing. Looking back, it's not a part of my past that I boast about, but I'm grateful for the chance to rewrite my story.

These days, I steer clear of hangovers like they're the plague. Not only do they wreak havoc on my blood sugar levels, but they also drain me of energy and joy. So, I've learned to keep my alcohol intake in check, opting for quality over quantity. A glass or two of white wine satisfies my cravings without sending my sugars on a rollercoaster ride. It's all about balancing and enjoying the simple pleasures in moderation.

Embracing the Good Ol' Days of Home Cooking

Growing up in a bustling household with eleven siblings, our go-to meals were as simple as they got—meat, two veggies, and the trusty potato. Dad, being a potato merchant, made sure we always had spuds!

Fast forward to today, and we're still all about that Sunday roast with all the trimmings. It's a tradition that brings us together and fills our bellies with warmth and love.

I've been around the block with diets - Slimming World, Weight Watchers, Scarsdale, you name it. But let's be honest, nothing beats a good home-cooked meal that doesn't mess with my blood sugar levels.

With a mountain of cookbooks and a family full of cooking pros, I do my best to whip up simple, quick dishes that hit the spot. These recipes keep us coming back for more, week in and week out, because, at the end of the day, it's all about good food, good company, and good times.

Celebrating the Mediterranean Flavors with a Twist

In our culinary journey, we've embraced the vibrant and wholesome Mediterranean-style diet. It's a love affair with fresh ingredients, bold flavours, and a touch of sunshine in every bite. Scrolling through Instagram feeds, exploring new recipes, and experimenting with innovative ideas has become a delightful pastime that keeps our taste buds tingling with anticipation.

But let's be honest - when it comes to cooking, I'm all about quick, easy, and bursting with flavour. These kinds of meals don't just fill your stomach but also make your taste buds do a little happy dance.

Now, here's the kicker: I've recently taken a break from garlic. Yep, you heard that right. So, if garlic sneaks into my meals, it better be playing hide-and-seek because I won't stand for its pungent presence - I'm talking about frying it until it's practically anonymous so I can enjoy the dish without the overpowering garlic taste.

With a newfound appreciation for Mediterranean cuisine and a knack for turning simple ingredients into culinary delights, I'm on a mission to create delicious dishes that cater to my evolving taste preferences. So, join me as we explore the colourful world of Mediterranean flavours with a dash of creativity and a pinch of garlic-free magic.

RECIPES

Stuffed Cajun Chicken

Ingredients

- 2 tbsp. extra-virgin olive oil
- 1 c. medium onion, diced
- 1 c. red and green bell pepper, diced
- Salt to taste
- Freshly ground black pepper
- 4 boneless, skinless chicken breasts
- 1 c. shredded cheddar
- 2 tbsp. Cajun seasoning

Method

1. Preheat oven to 350°. In a large ovenproof skillet over medium heat, heat oil. Add onions and peppers and cook until soft, 5 minutes. Season with salt and pepper. Remove from heat and let cool slightly.
2. With a sharp paring knife, create a pocket in each chicken breast. Stuff each with vegetable mixture, then top with cheddar. Season chicken all over with Cajun seasoning, salt, and pepper.
3. Add chicken to skillet and bake until cooked through for about 25 minutes.

RECIPES

Turkey Taco Lettuce Wraps

Ingredients

- 2 tbsp. extra-virgin olive oil
- 1 small yellow onion, chopped
- 1 lb. ground turkey
- 1 tsp. salt
- 1 tbsp. tomato paste
- 1 tbsp. chilli powder
- 2 heads romaine lettuce, outer leaves separated

For Serving

- Shredded cheese
- Chopped tomatoes
- Chopped red onion
- Chopped avocado or guacamole
- Freshly chopped coriander

Method

1. Heat oil in a large pan over medium-high. Add onion and cook until just soft, about 5 minutes. Add turkey and season with salt. Cook, breaking up meat with the side of a spoon, until meat is cooked through, 4 minutes.
2. Stir in tomato paste and chilli powder and cook for 1 minute.
3. Double up the lettuce leaves. Divide the meat mixture among the leaves. Sprinkle with cheese, tomato, onion, avocado, and coriander and serve.

RECIPES

Prawn Stir Fry

Ingredients

- 2 tbsp. extra-virgin olive oil
- 450 g raw king prawns, peeled and deveined
- Salt to taste
- Freshly ground black pepper
- 1 tbsp. sesame oil
- 1 small head broccoli, cut into small florets
- 200 g sugar snap peas
- 1 red pepper, sliced
- 3 cloves garlic, crushed
- 1 tbsp. crushed ginger
- 100 ml low-sodium soy sauce
- 1 tbsp. cornflour
- Juice of 1 lime
- 2 tbsp.
- Pinch chilli flakes

Method

1. Step 1In a large pan over medium heat, heat olive oil. Add prawns and season with salt and pepper. Cook until pink, 5 minutes, then remove from pan.
2. Return pan to heat and heat sesame oil. Add broccoli, peas, and pepper and cook until soft, 7 minutes. Add garlic and ginger and cook until fragrant, 1 minute more.
3. In a small bowl, whisk together soy sauce, cornflour, lime juice, and a pinch of chilli flakes. Add to pan and toss to coat. Add prawns and cook until heated through 2 minutes.

RECIPES

Lorraine's Yummy Chicken

Ingredients

- 3 tbsp. extra-virgin olive oil, divided
- 4 (8-oz.) boneless, skinless chicken breasts
- Salt to taste
- Freshly ground black pepper
- A tiny squeeze of lazy garlic
- Tbsp fresh thyme
- 1 tsp. crushed red pepper flakes or lazy chilli
- 3/4 cup chicken broth
- 1/2 cup chopped sun-dried tomatoes
- Some heavy cream
- 1/4 cup finely grated Parmesan
- Torn fresh basil for serving

Method

1. Preheat oven to 375°. In a large ovenproof pan over medium-high heat, heat 1 tablespoon oil. Generously season chicken with salt and black pepper and cook, turning halfway through, until golden brown, about 5 minutes per side. Transfer chicken to a plate.
2. In the same pan over medium heat, heat the remaining 2 tablespoons of oil. Stir in garlic, thyme, and red pepper flakes. Cook, stirring, until fragrant, about 1 minute. Stir in broth, tomatoes, cream, and Parmesan; season with salt. Bring to a simmer, then return the chicken and any accumulated juices to the pan.
3. Transfer skillet to oven. Bake chicken until cooked through and the juices run clear when pierced with a knife, 10 to 12 minutes.
4. Arrange chicken on a platter. Spoon sauce over. Top with basil.

RECIPES

One Pot Salmon & Asparagus

Ingredients

- 400g new potato, halved if large
- 2 tbsp olive oil
- 8 asparagus spears, trimmed and halved
- 2 handfuls cherry tomatoes
- 1 tbsp balsamic vinegar
- 2 salmon fillets, about 140g/5oz each
- handful basil leaves

Method

1. Heat oven to 220C/fan 200C/gas 7. Tip the potatoes and 1 tbsp of olive oil into an ovenproof dish, then roast the potatoes for 20 mins until starting to brown. Toss the asparagus in with the potatoes, then return to the oven for 15 mins.
2. Throw in the cherry tomatoes and vinegar and nestle the salmon amongst the vegetables. Drizzle with the remaining oil and return to the oven for a final 10-15 mins until the salmon is cooked. Scatter over the basil leaves and serve everything scooped straight from the dish.

RECIPES

Chicken Breast Over Asparagus

Ingredients

- 3 chicken breasts
- 1 lbs asparagus
- 5 oz cherry/grape tomatoes
- 1 cup Parmigiano Reggiano- freshly grated
- 1 tsp paprika
- 1 1/2 tsp salt
- a teeny squeeze of lazy garlic
- 1 tsp Italian seasoning
- Black pepper
- 1/4 cup olive oil
- Basil leaves, for garnish

Method

1. Pound chicken breast to help cook evenly; season with olive oil, paprika, Italian seasoning, garlic powder, salt and pepper on both sides and pan sear until internal temperature reaches 145- 150 F;
2. Preheat oven to 400 F;
3. Clean your asparagus and season with olive oil, salt and pepper; split into 3 parts and place each chicken breast on top; add cherry/grape tomatoes, season tomatoes with olive oil and salt and shred Parmigiano Reggiano on top;
4. Finish cooking in the oven for about 15 mins until internal temperature reaches 165 F;
5. Top with more Parmigiano Reggiano, black pepper, basil leaves and enjoy!

RECIPES

Chicken In Pan With Spinach & Tomatoes

Ingredients

- 2 tbsp olive oil
- 5 or 6 thinly sliced chicken breasts
- 3 garlic cloves
- 1 shallot
- 2 cups cherry tomatoes
- 3 cups spinach
- Large spoon of pesto
- 1/2 cup heavy cream
- 1/3 cup chicken stock
- Salt to taste
- Pepper
- Garlic powder
- Onion powder
- 1/2 tsp red pepper flakes

Method

1. Season the chicken with salt & pepper, garlic & chilli powder. I have the chicken flattened, so it takes less time.
2. Pan fry in a deep pan until golden. Then remove
3. In the same pan, then add tomatoes and shallots. Cook the tomatoes for a minutes, then add in spinach pesto and cream.
4. Then add the chicken back in and cook for another few minutes.

I serve it on its own for a no-carb meal, or we love a potato with it or some rice.

RECIPES

Chicken In Tortilla Wraps

Note: The wraps are cards so adjust accordingly)

Ingredients

- 4 medium skinless, boneless chicken thighs
- 1 large brown onion, cut into thick wedges
- 1 tsp each ground cumin, coriander, paprika
- ½ tsp ground cinnamon
- flake salt, fresh ground black pepper
- Zest ½ lemon
- 2 clove garlic, finely grated
- 1 tbsp extra virgin olive oil + extra for cooking

The Dressing

- 250g cottage cheese
- Handful mint, roughly chopped
- Juice ½ lemon
- Coriander
- Mint

The Salad to be Served on top

- 1 Lebanese sliced
- 1 small red onion finely sliced
- ¼ cup pickled chilis chopped
- Large handful parsley, mint, coriander, roughly chopped
- 1 tsp sumac
- Juice ½ lemon
- 2 tbsp extra virgin olive oil

RECIPES

Chicken In Tortilla Wraps (Continued)

Method

- Cut each chicken thigh into 3 pieces and combine with the onion, spices, lemon zest, 1 clove
- Add the garlic, salt, pepper and 1 tbsp of olive oil. Let this marinate for at least 30 minutes.
- In a small food processor or blender, combine the cottage cheese, remaining 1 clove garlic,
- Add the mint & lemon, fresh ground black pepper., coriander & mint. Blend to a smooth consistency. Set aside.
- In a bowl, combine the tomatoes, cucumbers, onion, chilis, herbs, sumac, lemon, olive oil. Season with salt & pepper to taste.
- Heat a large frying pan over a high heat and a good splash of olive oil and the marinated chicken and onions. Cook for 2 minutes then turn the chicken over and move everything around the pan so the onions are cooking evenly and caramelising. Cook for 2-3 minutes.

To Serve

Place the chicken onto the warm pitas, spoon over some of the salad, and finish with a big spoonful of the herbed cottage cheese. Serve with extra lemon wedges, if desired.

Quote

Diabetes is like a roller coaster. It has its ups and downs, but it's your choice to scream or enjoy the ride.

Unknown

Weekly Meal Planner and Diabetes Tracker

On the following pages, I have provided a weekly meal planner template that includes sections for tracking blood sugars, exercise details, insulin intake, mood, and sleep. You can use this as a starting point and customise it based on your preferences and daily routine.

Feel free to print multiple copies of this template for each day of the week and use it to plan your meals, track blood sugars, record exercise details, monitor insulin intake, note your mood, and track sleep patterns. This comprehensive tracker can help you stay organised, effectively manage your diabetes, and identify patterns or trends impacting your blood sugar control.

Remember to consult your healthcare provider or diabetes care team for personalised recommendations and adjustments to your meal plan and diabetes management routine. Consistent tracking and monitoring can provide valuable insights and support your efforts in maintaining reasonable blood sugar control and overall well-being.

Weekly Meal Planner and Diabetes Tracker
Week 1.

		Pre-Meal Blood Sugar	Carbs	Insulin Taken	Blood Sugar 2 hrs Later	Sleep & Mood	Exercise
MON	Breakfast					Hours Sleep:	Time:
	Snack					Mood: 😊 😊 😊	Type:
	Lunch						
	Dinner						
	Snack					😐 😞 😣	
TUE	Breakfast					Hours Sleep:	Time:
	Snack					Mood: 😊 😊 😊	Type:
	Lunch						
	Dinner						
	Snack					😐 😞 😣	
WED	Breakfast					Hours Sleep:	Time:
	Snack					Mood: 😊 😊 😊	Type:
	Lunch						
	Dinner						
	Snack					😐 😞 😣	
THU	Breakfast					Hours Sleep:	Time:
	Snack					Mood: 😊 😊 😊	Type:
	Lunch						
	Dinner						
	Snack					😐 😞 😣	
FRI	Breakfast					Hours Sleep:	Time:
	Snack					Mood: 😊 😊 😊	Type:
	Lunch						
	Dinner						
	Snack					😐 😞 😣	
SAT	Breakfast					Hours Sleep:	Time:
	Snack					Mood: 😊 😊 😊	Type:
	Lunch						
	Dinner						
	Snack					😐 😞 😣	
SUN	Breakfast					Hours Sleep:	Time:
	Snack					Mood: 😊 😊 😊	Type:
	Lunch						
	Dinner						
	Snack					😐 😞 😣	

Weekly Meal Planner and Diabetes Tracker
Week 2.

		Pre-Meal Blood Sugar	Carbs	Insulin Taken	Blood Sugar 2 hrs Later	Sleep & Mood	Exercise
MON	Breakfast					Hours Sleep:	Time:
	Snack					Mood:	Type:
	Lunch					😀 🙂 😐	
	Dinner						
	Snack					😕 😟 😞	
TUE	Breakfast					Hours Sleep:	Time:
	Snack					Mood:	Type:
	Lunch					😀 🙂 😐	
	Dinner						
	Snack					😕 😟 😞	
WED	Breakfast					Hours Sleep:	Time:
	Snack					Mood:	Type:
	Lunch					😀 🙂 😐	
	Dinner						
	Snack					😕 😟 😞	
THU	Breakfast					Hours Sleep:	Time:
	Snack					Mood:	Type:
	Lunch					😀 🙂 😐	
	Dinner						
	Snack					😕 😟 😞	
FRI	Breakfast					Hours Sleep:	Time:
	Snack					Mood:	Type:
	Lunch					😀 🙂 😐	
	Dinner						
	Snack					😕 😟 😞	
SAT	Breakfast					Hours Sleep:	Time:
	Snack					Mood:	Type:
	Lunch					😀 🙂 😐	
	Dinner						
	Snack					😕 😟 😞	
SUN	Breakfast					Hours Sleep:	Time:
	Snack					Mood:	Type:
	Lunch					😀 🙂 😐	
	Dinner						
	Snack					😕 😟 😞	

Weekly Meal Planner and Diabetes Tracker
Week 3.

		Pre-Meal Blood Sugar	Carbs	Insulin Taken	Blood Sugar 2 hrs Later	Sleep & Mood	Exercise
MON	Breakfast					Hours Sleep:	Time:
	Snack					Mood:	Type:
	Lunch						
	Dinner						
	Snack						
TUE	Breakfast					Hours Sleep:	Time:
	Snack					Mood:	Type:
	Lunch						
	Dinner						
	Snack						
WED	Breakfast					Hours Sleep:	Time:
	Snack					Mood:	Type:
	Lunch						
	Dinner						
	Snack						
THU	Breakfast					Hours Sleep:	Time:
	Snack					Mood:	Type:
	Lunch						
	Dinner						
	Snack						
FRI	Breakfast					Hours Sleep:	Time:
	Snack					Mood:	Type:
	Lunch						
	Dinner						
	Snack						
SAT	Breakfast					Hours Sleep:	Time:
	Snack					Mood:	Type:
	Lunch						
	Dinner						
	Snack						
SUN	Breakfast					Hours Sleep:	Time:
	Snack					Mood:	Type:
	Lunch						
	Dinner						
	Snack						

Weekly Meal Planner and Diabetes Tracker
Week 4.

		Pre-Meal Blood Sugar	Carbs	Insulin Taken	Blood Sugar 2 hrs Later	Sleep & Mood	Exercise
MON	Breakfast					Hours Sleep:	Time:
	Snack					Mood:	Type:
	Lunch						
	Dinner						
	Snack						
TUE	Breakfast					Hours Sleep:	Time:
	Snack					Mood:	Type:
	Lunch						
	Dinner						
	Snack						
WED	Breakfast					Hours Sleep:	Time:
	Snack					Mood:	Type:
	Lunch						
	Dinner						
	Snack						
THU	Breakfast					Hours Sleep:	Time:
	Snack					Mood:	Type:
	Lunch						
	Dinner						
	Snack						
FRI	Breakfast					Hours Sleep:	Time:
	Snack					Mood:	Type:
	Lunch						
	Dinner						
	Snack						
SAT	Breakfast					Hours Sleep:	Time:
	Snack					Mood:	Type:
	Lunch						
	Dinner						
	Snack						
SUN	Breakfast					Hours Sleep:	Time:
	Snack					Mood:	Type:
	Lunch						
	Dinner						
	Snack						

Weekly Meal Planner and Diabetes Tracker
Week 5.

		Pre-Meal Blood Sugar	Carbs	Insulin Taken	Blood Sugar 2 hrs Later	Sleep & Mood	Exercise
MON	Breakfast					Hours Sleep:	Time:
	Snack					Mood:	Type:
	Lunch					😃 🙂 😊	
	Dinner						
	Snack					😐 ☹️ 😣	
TUE	Breakfast					Hours Sleep:	Time:
	Snack					Mood:	Type:
	Lunch					😃 🙂 😊	
	Dinner						
	Snack					😐 ☹️ 😣	
WED	Breakfast					Hours Sleep:	Time:
	Snack					Mood:	Type:
	Lunch					😃 🙂 😊	
	Dinner						
	Snack					😐 ☹️ 😣	
THU	Breakfast					Hours Sleep:	Time:
	Snack					Mood:	Type:
	Lunch					😃 🙂 😊	
	Dinner						
	Snack					😐 ☹️ 😣	
FRI	Breakfast					Hours Sleep:	Time:
	Snack					Mood:	Type:
	Lunch					😃 🙂 😊	
	Dinner						
	Snack					😐 ☹️ 😣	
SAT	Breakfast					Hours Sleep:	Time:
	Snack					Mood:	Type:
	Lunch					😃 🙂 😊	
	Dinner						
	Snack					😐 ☹️ 😣	
SUN	Breakfast					Hours Sleep:	Time:
	Snack					Mood:	Type:
	Lunch					😃 🙂 😊	
	Dinner						
	Snack					😐 ☹️ 😣	

Chapter 13

More Hints and Tips to Help You on Your Journey

Type 1 diabetes was previously known as juvenile diabetes, and it is mainly diagnosed in children or teenagers. However, around 25% of people with type 1 diabetes may not be diagnosed until they reach adulthood, with some being diagnosed as late as 80 or 90 years old. Although there is no cure for this condition, there are steps you can take to make it more manageable as an adult.

Find the Right Teammates

It's essential for individuals with diabetes to have a personalised plan in place. However, creating this plan doesn't have to be a solo effort. It's beneficial to consult with a team of healthcare professionals, including a general physician, an endocrinologist, a nutritionist or dietitian, and a diabetes educator. Depending on your situation, you may also need to see other specialists, such as a podiatrist for your feet and lower legs or an ophthalmologist for your eyes.

To ensure that you're taking the best possible care of your health, it's important to communicate regularly with your healthcare team and keep them informed about your condition.

Understand the Possible Problems

It's important to keep an eye on your blood sugar levels since high blood sugar can lead to issues with organs and tissues in your body. Even if you are managing your diabetes well, problems can still arise over time. Make sure to get checked regularly and look out for warning signs such as tingling, numbness, or swelling in your hands and feet, blurred or double vision, or sores that don't heal. Early detection and treatment of these issues can help slow down or even prevent further damage.

Eat Well, and Eat Often

It is recommended that instead of having three large meals in a day, you should eat small amounts of food at regular intervals. To keep your blood sugar steady, you should consult your dietitian about the best food choices. Your dietitian may suggest healthy fats such as nuts, protein-rich foods like lean meat, fish or beans, whole grains like brown rice or oatmeal, and colourful veggies like spinach, peppers, broccoli, and sweet potatoes. In addition, low-calorie drinks like unsweetened iced tea or water flavoured with fresh fruit can also be a good option.

Regular exercise has numerous benefits such as helping to reduce weight, maintaining healthy blood sugar levels, and lowering blood pressure. Additionally, it can also protect you from eye or kidney problems. However, it is important to keep a close watch on your blood sugar levels before, during, and after a workout, since exercise can increase or decrease your levels and may even lead to dangerously low blood sugar or hypoglycemia. It is essential to understand how exercise can affect your blood sugar and take the necessary medication or eat accordingly.

It's important to get vaccinated if you have diabetes, as it can weaken your immune system and make it harder for your body to fight infections. Some infections, such as the flu, can also cause your blood sugar to rise. Adults with type 1 diabetes should stay up to date on their vaccinations, which include getting a yearly flu shot, as well as the hepatitis B vaccine, pneumococcal vaccine (to protect against pneumonia), zoster vaccine (to protect against shingles), and TDAP vaccine (to protect against tetanus, diphtheria, and whooping cough).

Keeping track of what you eat, regularly pricking your fingers for blood sugar tests, and monitoring insulin injections can get tedious and monotonous, especially if you have been doing it every day for years or even decades. You are bound to face setbacks, as even something as minor as changing the location of your insulin shot or tweaking the recipe of your favourite dish can bring unexpected results. It is important to acknowledge that achieving perfect control is not always possible, and not to let those bad days derail your progress.

If you are dealing with type 1 diabetes, it can be beneficial to connect with others who are going through a similar situation. You can ask your doctor or diabetes educator about meetings, support groups, or sessions where you can meet other adults with type 1 diabetes. Moreover, if you are experiencing symptoms of depression, such as loss of interest in activities you used to enjoy, extremely low energy, or hopelessness, it is advisable to seek professional support.

Chapter 14
Talking About Diabetes Language Matters

The Diabetes Language Matters movement supports better communication with and about those living with diabetes. It is not a new concept; it started in Australia in 2011, and since then, many countries have followed suit with their own versions of guides and position statements. See: https://www.languagemattersdiabetes.com/

Diabetes is a complex condition affecting approximately 300,000 people in Ireland. No one causes their diabetes, yet people living with diabetes often encounter stigma, discrimination, and being stereotyped. There is plenty of evidence to suggest we can improve our messaging, body language, and spoken word to be more supportive of the person living with diabetes. So, how we speak and write about diabetes matters!

In early 2023, the Diabetes Language Matters Ireland Working Group came together to develop an Irish version of a Diabetes Language Matters guide. This group consists of people with lived experience of diabetes, academics, and healthcare professionals.

This short Irish Language Matters guide aims to raise awareness of how improving communication with and about people with diabetes can make a difference in supporting people living with the condition. It was developed to support people working in the media as well as the general public in Ireland.

Why Diabetes Language Matters

The evidence suggests that the words used to describe diabetes and people with diabetes have an impact on both the emotional and physical well-being of those living with the condition.

Words have the power to both heal and harm. They can create a space that is both positive, where a person can feel supported and understood, or negative, where they can feel stigmatised, undervalued, blamed, and misunderstood.

Many of us have not considered or realised the influence our words can have. We often do not reflect on whether we express a conscious or unconscious bias. Yet, how we communicate can have a profound effect on outcomes, self-management, and experience of healthcare for the person living with diabetes.

There is a lot of evidence demonstrating how words impact the person living with diabetes

- Language used in the media can be stigmatising.

- Language used at diagnosis has a lasting impact on the person with diabetes.

- Language around diabetes can be confusing, inaccurate, unrealistic and harmful.

- Language affects self-management. For example, during a clinic experience, a person can feel supported, understood and confident or belittled, criticised and patronised.

- Language around diabetes can affect emotional well-being. People with diabetes report feelings of guilt, frustration, and anxiety around blood glucose levels and food choices which may be triggered by the language they hear around self-management.

➢ Language contributes to social stigma which can include unhelpful comments and judgement leading to diabetes distress, depression and lowered self-esteem.

➢ Language affects self-care, for example attending medical appointments and taking medication.

➢ Language affects clinicians' attitudes.

➢ Language isolates people affected by diabetes leading to loneliness.

Recommended Language

It is recommended that language be:

- Person-centred.

- Free of stigma.

- Neutral, non-judgmental, and based on evidence.

- Strengths-based, respectful, and inclusive.

- Collaborative with the person living with diabetes.

- When talking about diabetes in the media we ask that the messaging be trustworthy, reliable, honest, caring, and compassionate.

- Avoid using blameful language like "failed to control" or "non-compliant." Diabetes management is complex and influenced by various factors.

- Recognise the daily efforts of people with diabetes in managing their condition.

- Be understanding about the challenges people with diabetes face and the constant need for monitoring and decision-making.

- Using words like "be healthier" instead of "be healthy" takes away any assumption a person does not have any health promoting behaviours.

Example of Insensitive Things People Say / Do to People with Diabetes

"I get asked "Are you allowed to eat that?" or "Should you be eating that you can't eat sugar", all the time.
Once a friend snatched the bar, I was using to treat a hypo out of my hand and threw it in the bin."

Quote From Someone with Diabetes

"When I see diabetes represented in such a simplistic way in newspapers, I get so annoyed. It's such a complicated condition to manage, it really isn't just about diet and exercise and usually, what is headlined as a life-changing therapy really isn't."

Example of Insensitive Things People Say to People with Diabetes

"You really should be trying to lose some weight, aren't you going to put your baby at risk?"

Examples of Language in the Media

✗ Typical Headlines:

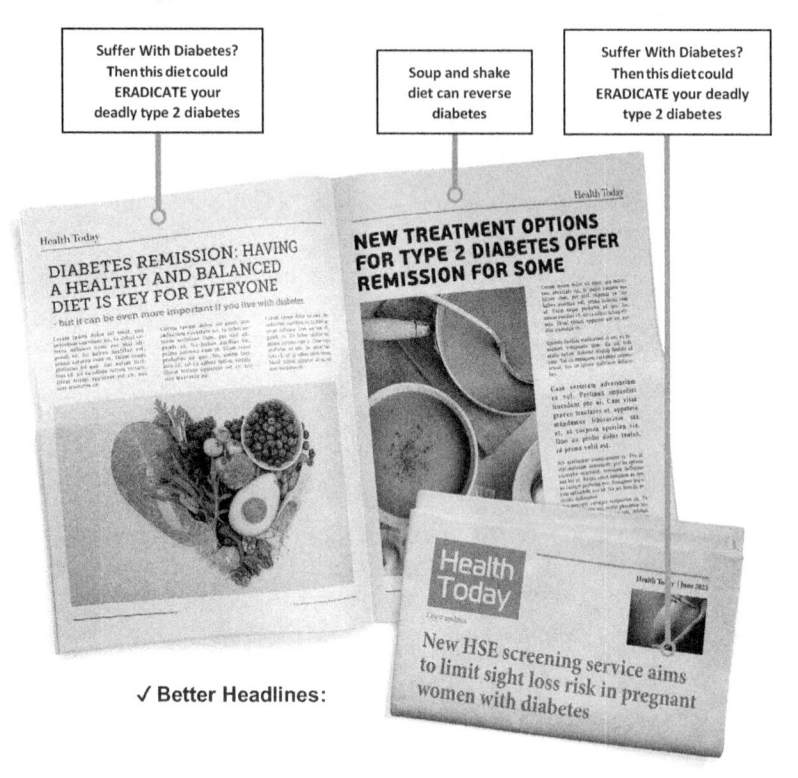

> Suffer With Diabetes? Then this diet could ERADICATE your deadly type 2 diabetes

> Soup and shake diet can reverse diabetes

> Suffer With Diabetes? Then this diet could ERADICATE your deadly type 2 diabetes

✓ Better Headlines:

> DIABETES REMISSION: HAVING A HEALTHY AND BALANCED DIET IS KEY FOR EVERYONE - but it can be even more important if you live with diabetes

> NEW TREATMENT OPTIONS FOR TYPE 2 DIABETES OFFER REMISSION FOR SOME

> New HSE screening service aims to limit sight loss risk in pregnant women with diabetes

If you write or speak about diabetes or know someone living with diabetes, please think about your use of words and consider using some of the suggested alternatives below.

Words / Phrases to Avoid	Preferred Language	Why?
'Diabetic'	Ask individuals if they prefer diabetic or person with diabetes. If this is not possible, using Person/People with Diabetes is preferred.	A Person with Diabetes is not defined by their condition. Put the person first to avoid using their condition to describe them.
Sufferer 'Suffering' from or with diabetes.	Person living with diabetes (PLwD): While some people may find diabetes management and its complications challenging and distressing, not everyone 'suffers' with diabetes.	Referring to people with diabetes as "diabetic sufferers' positions them as helpless victims, unable to lead a normal life with diabetes.
Patient (If not an inpatient and/ or outside of the clinic context).	Person living with diabetes or as above or with lived experience/ service user.	The term 'Patient' implies they are passively receiving care rather than being actively involved in their own care. Patients are people, and people are individuals, with their own preferences, priorities and lives beyond diabetes.

Words / Phrases to Avoid	Preferred Language	Why?
Non-diabetic / Normal / Healthy (to describe those without diabetes).	Person without diabetes.	The opposite of normal is abnormal, and people with diabetes are most definitely not 'abnormal'.
Compliant or non-compliance 'He is non-compliant with taking his insulin'.	Engaged/ involved. 'He takes his medication when he is reminded using his app'. His/Her diabetes management plan is not working for them at the moment.	Diabetes relies on self-management; it involves collaboration between the healthcare team and the Person with Diabetes. The aim is to focus on what someone does well and how this can be built on.
Diabetes can be 'reversed' or put into remission (Avoid making general statements about diabetes without stating which type you are referring to)	Always make sure to state which type of diabetes you are referring to when making broad statements otherwise this could be misleading and inaccurate.	Type 2 diabetes remission is possible in some cases, but may not be feasible for all. Type 1 diabetes cannot be put into remission.

Words / Phrases to Avoid	Preferred Language	Why?
In relation to the topic of **"Diabetes complications"**, avoid using scaremongering words such as **"killer/deadly disease"**. At risk of going blind from this 'deadly' disease	Raised glucose levels over time can pose a risk for a number of complications.	Avoid scaremongering or using terms that have overtly negative tones. The term complications is complex, unclear and may be fear-inducing. The key is to raise awareness and focus on prevention, health checks, detection and treatment plans.

Summary

Language will continue to evolve as our understanding of all types of diabetes grows.

Harmful, stigmatising words are mostly unintentional. It can take time to change our language and while we highlight the need for change it should always be done in a non-accusatory manner particularly on social media.

Stay informed and open. Keep up to date by referring to guidelines by reputable organisations and keep listening to the diabetes community.

Contributors to the Information on Language Matters:

Susie Birney - PLwD, ICPO, Cathy Breen - HSE National Clinical Programme for Diabetes,

Ann-Marie Creaven - University of Limerick, Sonya Deschênes - University College Dublin, Gráinne Flynn - PLwD, Thriveabetes,

Tomás Griffin - University of Galway and Galway University Hospitals,

Cameron Keighron - PLwD, University of Galway,

Joanne Lowe - HSE National Clinical Programme for Diabetes,

Michelle Lowry - PLwD, Occupational Therapist,

Amy McInerney - University College Dublin, Eimear Morrisey - University of Galway, Sinéad Powell - Diabetes Ireland

Chapter 15

Final Words – My Formula for Wellness

As I reflect on the 28 years of my life with diabetes, one thing stands out above all else: the power of embracing both the highs and lows, and finding balance amidst the storm. My story is not just about managing type 1 diabetes; it's about navigating the complexities of life with resilience, innovation, and unwavering determination.

At the heart of my journey lies a simple equation: Managing insulin plus food, plus emotion equals good control. But the last component, emotion, has truly been the driving force behind my success. For years, I struggled to find stability amidst the chaos of fluctuating blood sugar levels and the emotional toll it took on me. It wasn't until I addressed my emotions head-on, with the support of my healthcare team that I truly began to thrive. Now, with the aid of revolutionary technology like the T Slim Pump powered by AI, things have become even better.

I want to emphasise to anyone facing similar challenges that while technology is a game-changer, emotional well-being determines the quality of life. Once I mastered the art of managing my emotions, everything else fell into place. The AI may have sorted out the technical aspects, but my emotional resilience and determination paved the way for my brighter future.

As I look forward to the adventures that lie ahead, I am filled with gratitude for the life I've been given. Despite the hurdles I've faced, I love every moment, cherishing each experience as an opportunity for growth and self-discovery. My journey has taught me to embrace innovation, to remain at the forefront of technology, and to never stop pushing for better solutions.

So, to anyone out there struggling with diabetes or any other challenge, I urge you to embrace your journey with open arms. Keep innovating, keep pushing the boundaries, and above all, take care of your emotional well-being. Ultimately, it's not just about managing a condition; it's about crafting a life filled with purpose, joy, and endless possibilities.

This is my story, my journey, and I hope it serves as a beacon of inspiration for anyone embarking on their own path to wellness. Embrace technology, harness the power of your emotions, and never stop believing in the incredible potential that lies within you. The journey may be challenging, but the destination is worth every step of the way.

Acknowledgement
For Rachel McDarby

As a tribute to your memory and the indelible mark you left upon my journey. Though your time among us was fleeting, your name resonates through the annals of time, a testament to the enduring power of the human spirit.

Your death was cruel and untimely, but it served as a catalyst, propelling me to seize each moment with renewed vigour and embrace life in all its kaleidoscopic splendour.

Rachel McDarby

> # *Quote*
>
> Food + AI + Emotion = A Very Happy and Balanced Person Living with Type I Diabetes.
>
> Lorraine Sweeney

NOTES

NOTES

NOTES

NOTES

NOTES

NOTES

NOTES

NOTES

NOTES

NOTES

NOTES

NOTES

NOTES

NOTES

NOTES

NOTES

NOTES

NOTES

NOTES

NOTES

NOTES

NOTES

NOTES

NOTES

NOTES

NOTES

NOTES

NOTES

NOTES

NOTES

NOTES

NOTES

NOTES

NOTES

NOTES

NOTES

NOTES

NOTES

NOTES

Let Us Connect

Please feel free to get in touch or look me up on social media!

@SweetSugarPump

Printed in Great Britain
by Amazon